With Cram101.com online, you also have access to extensive reference material.

You will nail those essays and papers. Here is an example from a Cram101 Biology text:

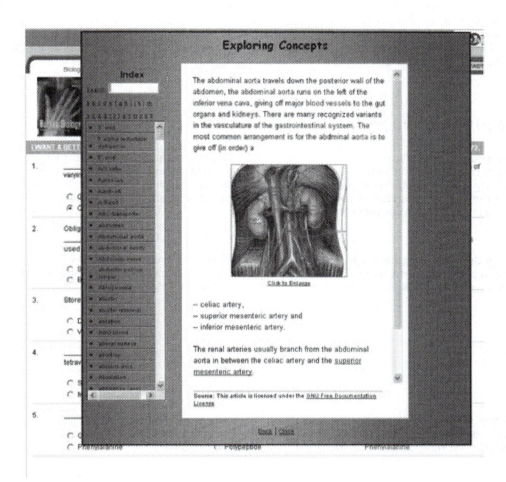

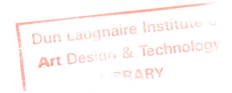
Learning System

Cram101 Textbook Outlines is a learning system. The notes in this book are the highlights of your textbook, you will never have to highlight a book again.

How to use this book. Take this book to class, it is your notebook for the lecture. The notes and highlights on the left hand side of the pages follow the outline and order of the textbook. All you have to do is follow along while your intructor presents the lecture. Circle the items emphasized in class and add other important information on the right side. With Cram101 Textbook Outlines you'll spend less time writing and more time listening. Learning becomes more efficient.

Cram101.com Online

Increase your studying efficiency by using Cram101.com's practice tests and online reference material. It is the perfect complement to Cram101 Textbook Outlines. Use self-teaching matching tests or simulate in-class testing with comprehensive multiple choice tests, or simply use Cram's true and false tests for quick review. Cram101.com even allows you to enter your in-class notes for an integrated studying format combining the textbook notes with your class notes.

Visit **www.Cram101.com**, click Sign Up at the top of the screen, and enter **DK73DW414** in the promo code box on the registration screen. Access to www.Cram101.com is normally $9.95, but because you have purchased this book, your access fee is only $4.95. Sign up and stop highlighting textbooks forever.

Cram101 Textbook Outlines to accompany:

Strategic Planning for Information Systems

Ward and Peppard, 3rd Edition

An Academic Internet Publishers (AIPI) publication (c) 2007.

You have a discounted membership at www.Cram101.com with this book.

Get all of the practice tests for the chapters of this textbook, and access in-depth reference material for writing essays and papers. Here is an example from a Cram101 Biology text:

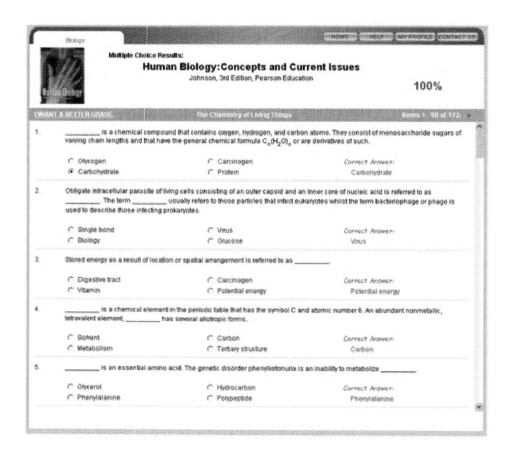

When you need problem solving help with math, stats, and other disciplines, www.Cram101.com will walk through the formulas and solutions step by step.

Strategic Planning for Information Systems
Ward and Peppard, 3rd

CONTENTS

Information technology	Information technology refers to technology that helps companies change business by allowing them to use new methods.
Technology	The body of knowledge and techniques that can be used to combine economic resources to produce goods and services is called technology.
Industry	A group of firms that produce identical or similar products is an industry. It is also used specifically to refer to an area of economic production focused on manufacturing which involves large amounts of capital investment before any profit can be realized, also called "heavy industry".
Service	Service refers to a "non tangible product" that is not embodied in a physical good and that typically effects some change in another product, person, or institution. Contrasts with good.
Information system	An information system is a system whether automated or manual, that comprises people, machines, and/or methods organized to collect, process, transmit, and disseminate data that represent user information.
Investment	Investment refers to spending for the production and accumulation of capital and additions to inventories. In a financial sense, buying an asset with the expectation of making a return.
Insurance	Insurance refers to a system by which individuals can reduce their exposure to risk of large losses by spreading the risks among a large number of persons.
Strategic management	A philosophy of management that links strategic planning with dayto-day decision making. Strategic management seeks a fit between an organization's external and internal environments.
Management	Management characterizes the process of leading and directing all or part of an organization, often a business, through the deployment and manipulation of resources. Early twentieth-century management writer Mary Parker Follett defined management as "the art of getting things done through people."
Assessment	Collecting information and providing feedback to employees about their behavior, communication style, or skills is an assessment.
Acquisition	A company's purchase of the property and obligations of another company is an acquisition.
Convergence	The blending of various facets of marketing functions and communication technology to create more efficient and expanded synergies is a convergence.
Union	A worker association that bargains with employers over wages and working conditions is called a union.
Innovation	Innovation refers to the first commercially successful introduction of a new product, the use of a new method of production, or the creation of a new form of business organization.
Dell Computer	Dell Computer, formerly PC's Limited, was founded on the principle that by selling personal computer systems directly to customers, PC's Limited could best understand their needs and provide the most effective computing solutions to meet those needs.
Intervention	Intervention refers to an activity in which a government buys or sells its currency in the foreign exchange market in order to affect its currency's exchange rate.
Configuration	An organization's shape, which reflects the division of labor and the means of coordinating the divided tasks is configuration.
Option	A contract that gives the purchaser the option to buy or sell the underlying financial instrument at a specified price, called the exercise price or strike price, within a specific period of time.
Purchase order	A form on which items or services needed by a business firm are specified and then communicated to the vendor is a purchase order.
Confirmed	When the seller's bank agrees to assume liability on the letter of credit issued by the buyer's bank the transaction is confirmed.The term means that the credit is not only backed up by the issuing foreign bank, but that payment is also guaranteed by the notifying American bank.
Electronic mail	Electronic mail refers to electronic written communication between individuals using computers

3

	connected to the Internet.
Accounting	A system that collects and processes financial information about an organization and reports that information to decision makers is referred to as accounting.
Production	The creation of finished goods and services using the factors of production: land, labor, capital, entrepreneurship, and knowledge.
Enterprise resource planning	Computer-based production and operations system that links multiple firms into one integrated production unit is enterprise resource planning.
Enterprise	Enterprise refers to another name for a business organization. Other similar terms are business firm, sometimes simply business, sometimes simply firm, as well as company, and entity.
Vendor	A person who sells property to a vendee is a vendor. The words vendor and vendee are more commonly applied to the seller and purchaser of real estate, and the words seller and buyer are more commonly applied to the seller and purchaser of personal property.
Points	Loan origination fees that may be deductible as interest by a buyer of property. A seller of property who pays points reduces the selling price by the amount of the points paid for the buyer.
Oracle	In 2004, sales at Oracle grew at a rate of 14.5% to $6.2 billion, giving it 41.3% and the top share of the relational-database market. Their main competitors in the database arena are IBM DB2 and Microsoft SQL Server, and to a lesser extent Sybase, Teradata, Informix, and MySQL. In the applications arena, their main competitor is SAP.
Baan	In 1998 the Baan Corporation was exposed to be manipulating profits in a prelude to the big accounting scandals that marked the turn of the century. First Paul Baan left the company as a result of this, shortly after to be followed by brother Jan. The loss of confidence in the Baan Corporation was reflected in a rapidly declining share of the BaaN program in the ERP market.
Commerce	Commerce is the exchange of something of value between two entities. It is the central mechanism from which capitalism is derived.
Electronic data interchange	Electronic data interchange refers to the direct exchange between organizations of data via a computer-to-computer interface.
Electronic commerce	Electronic commerce or e-commerce, refers to any activity that uses some form of electronic communication in the inventory, exchange, advertisement, distribution, and payment of goods and services.
Exchange	The trade of things of value between buyer and seller so that each is better off after the trade is called the exchange.
Invoice	The itemized bill for a transaction, stating the nature of the transaction and its cost. In international trade, the invoice price is often the preferred basis for levying an ad valorem tariff.
Administration	Administration refers to the management and direction of the affairs of governments and institutions; a collective term for all policymaking officials of a government; the execution and implementation of public policy.
United Nations	An international organization created by multilateral treaty in 1945 to promote social and economic cooperation among nations and to protect human rights is the United Nations.
Automation	Automation allows machines to do work previously accomplished by people.
Browser	A program that allows a user to connect to the World Wide Web by simply typing in a URL is a browser.
Business model	A business model is the instrument by which a business intends to generate revenue and profits. It is a summary of how a company means to serve its employees and customers, and involves both strategy (what an business intends to do) as well as an implementation.

Manufacturing	Production of goods primarily by the application of labor and capital to raw materials and other intermediate inputs, in contrast to agriculture, mining, forestry, fishing, and services a manufacturing.
Logistics	Those activities that focus on getting the right amount of the right products to the right place at the right time at the lowest possible cost is referred to as logistics.
Retailing	All activities involved in selling, renting, and providing goods and services to ultimate consumers for personal, family, or household use is referred to as retailing.
Press release	A written public news announcement normally distributed to major news services is referred to as press release.
Shareholder value	For a publicly traded company, shareholder value is the part of its capitalization that is equity as opposed to long-term debt. In the case of only one type of stock, this would roughly be the number of outstanding shares times current shareprice.
Shareholder	A shareholder is an individual or company (including a corporation) that legally owns one or more shares of stock in a joined stock company.
Firm	An organization that employs resources to produce a good or service for profit and owns and operates one or more plants is referred to as a firm.
NASDAQ	NASDAQ is an American electronic stock exchange. It was founded in 1971 by the National Association of Securities Dealers who divested it in a series of sales in 2000 and 2001.
Economy	The income, expenditures, and resources that affect the cost of running a business and household are called an economy.
Brand	A name, symbol, or design that identifies the goods or services of one seller or group of sellers and distinguishes them from the goods and services of competitors is a brand.
Asset	An item of property, such as land, capital, money, a share in ownership, or a claim on others for future payment, such as a bond or a bank deposit is an asset.
Market	A market is, as defined in economics, a social arrangement that allows buyers and sellers to discover information and carry out a voluntary exchange of goods or services.
Business strategy	Business strategy, which refers to the aggregated operational strategies of single business firm or that of an SBU in a diversified corporation refers to the way in which a firm competes in its chosen arenas.
New economy	New economy, this term was used in the late 1990's to suggest that globalization and/or innovations in information technology had changed the way that the world economy works.
Enabling	Enabling refers to giving workers the education and tools they need to assume their new decision-making powers.
Inventory	Tangible property held for sale in the normal course of business or used in producing goods or services for sale is an inventory.
Data processing	Data processing refers to a name for business technology in the 1970s; included technology that supported an existing business and was primarily used to improve the flow of financial information.
Strategic planning	The process of determining the major goals of the organization and the policies and strategies for obtaining and using resources to achieve those goals is called strategic planning.
Management control	That aspect of management concerned with the comparison of actual versus planned performance as well as the development and implementation of procedures to correct substandard performance is called management control.
Bill of	A bill of materials describes a product in terms of its assemblies, sub-assemblies, and basic parts.

materials	Basically consisting of a list of parts, a bill of materials is an essential part of the design and manufacture of any product.
Bill of material	A bill of material is a list of all the materials needed to manufacture a product or product component.
Purchase ledger	A purchase ledger contains the personal accounts of suppliers from whom the business has bought on credit. (The creditors.) It records information such as invoices received, credit notes received and payments sent.
Ledger	Ledger refers to a specialized accounting book in which information from accounting journals is accumulated into specific categories and posted so that managers can find all the information about one account in the same place.
Stock	In financial terminology, stock is the capital raized by a corporation, through the issuance and sale of shares.
Portfolio	In finance, a portfolio is a collection of investments held by an institution or a private individual. Holding but not always a portfolio is part of an investment and risk-limiting strategy called diversification. By owning several assets, certain types of risk (in particular specific risk) can be reduced.
Maturity	Maturity refers to the final payment date of a loan or other financial instrument, after which point no further interest or principal need be paid.
Interest	In finance and economics, interest is the price paid by a borrower for the use of a lender's money. In other words, interest is the amount of paid to "rent" money for a period of time.
Integration	Economic integration refers to reducing barriers among countries to transactions and to movements of goods, capital, and labor, including harmonization of laws, regulations, and standards. Integrated markets theoretically function as a unified market.
Users	Users refer to people in the organization who actually use the product or service purchased by the buying center.
Marketing	Promoting and selling products or services to customers, or prospective customers, is referred to as marketing.
Expense	In accounting, an expense represents an event in which an asset is used up or a liability is incurred. In terms of the accounting equation, expenses reduce owners' equity.
Driving force	The key external pressure that will shape the future for an organization is a driving force. The driving force in an industry are the main underlying causes of changing industry and competitive conditions.
Credibility	The extent to which a source is perceived as having knowledge, skill, or experience relevant to a communication topic and can be trusted to give an unbiased opinion or present objective information on the issue is called credibility.
Senior management	Senior management is generally a team of individuals at the highest level of organizational management who have the day-to-day responsibilities of managing a corporation.
Reorganization	Reorganization occurs, among other instances, when one corporation acquires another in a merger or acquisition, a single corporation divides into two or more entities, or a corporation makes a substantial change in its capital structure.
Coalition	An informal alliance among managers who support a specific goal is called coalition.
Hierarchy	A system of grouping people in an organization according to rank from the top down in which all subordinate managers must report to one person is called a hierarchy.
Foundation	A Foundation is a type of philanthropic organization set up by either individuals or institutions as a legal entity (either as a corporation or trust) with the purpose of distributing grants to support

causes in line with the goals of the foundation.

Control system	A control system is a device or set of devices that manage the behavior of other devices. Some devices or systems are not controllable. A control system is an interconnection of components connected or related in such a manner as to command, direct, or regulate itself or another system.
Useful life	The length of service of a productive facility or piece of equipment is its useful life. The period of time during which an asset will have economic value and be usable.
Liability	A liability is a present obligation of the enterprise arizing from past events, the settlement of which is expected to result in an outflow from the enterprise of resources embodying economic benefits.
Comprehensive	A comprehensive refers to a layout accurate in size, color, scheme, and other necessary details to show how a final ad will look. For presentation only, never for reproduction.
Return on investment	Return on investment refers to the return a businessperson gets on the money he and other owners invest in the firm; for example, a business that earned $100 on a $1,000 investment would have a ROI of 10 percent: 100 divided by 1000.
Yield	The interest rate that equates a future value or an annuity to a given present value is a yield.
Performance improvement	Performance improvement is the concept of measuring the output of a particular process or procedure then modifying the process or procedure in order to increase the output, increase efficiency, or increase the effectiveness of the process or procedure.
Inventory management	The planning, coordinating, and controlling activities related to the flow of inventory into, through, and out of an organization is referred to as inventory management.
Business process	Business process refers to the individual activities of an enterprise. Processes can be viewed at a high level, for example, 'marketing,' or at the level of detailed subprocesses, for example, 'customer retention.'.
Warehouse	Warehouse refers to a location, often decentralized, that a firm uses to store, consolidate, age, or mix stock; house product-recall programs; or ease tax burdens.
Market share	That fraction of an industry's output accounted for by an individual firm or group of firms is called market share.
Auction	A preexisting business model that operates successfully on the Internet by announcing an item for sale and permitting multiple purchasers to bid on them under specified rules and condition is an auction.
Buyer	A buyer refers to a role in the buying center with formal authority and responsibility to select the supplier and negotiate the terms of the contract.
Exporter	A firm that sells its product in another country is an exporter.
Competitive advantage	A business is said to have a competitive advantage when its unique strengths, often based on cost, quality, time, and innovation, offer consumers a greater percieved value and there by diffentiating it from its competitors.
Restructuring	Restructuring is the corporate management term for the act of partially dismantling and reorganizing a company for the purpose of making it more efficient and therefore more profitable.
Specialist	A specialist is a trader who makes a market in one or several stocks and holds the limit order book for those stocks.
Relational database	Relational database refers to a database structure that stores information in separate files that can be linked by common elements.
Productivity	Productivity refers to the total output of goods and services in a given period of time divided by work hours.
Policy	Similar to a script in that a policy can be a less than completely rational decision-making method.

Go to **Cram101.com** for the Practice Tests for this Chapter.

	Involves the use of a pre-existing set of decision steps for any problem that presents itself.
Matching	Matching refers to an accounting concept that establishes when expenses are recognized. Expenses are matched with the revenues they helped to generate and are recognized when those revenues are recognized.
Extension	Extension refers to an out-of-court settlement in which creditors agree to allow the firm more time to meet its financial obligations. A new repayment schedule will be developed, subject to the acceptance of creditors.
Organization structure	The system of task, reporting, and authority relationships within which the organization does its work is referred to as the organization structure.
Contribution	In business organization law, the cash or property contributed to a business by its owners is referred to as contribution.
Economics	The social science dealing with the use of scarce resources to obtain the maximum satisfaction of society's virtually unlimited economic wants is an economics.
Gain	In finance, gain is a profit or an increase in value of an investment such as a stock or bond. Gain is calculated by fair market value or the proceeds from the sale of the investment minus the sum of the purchase price and all costs associated with it.
Project management	Project management is the discipline of organizing and managing resources in such a way that these resources deliver all the work required to complete a project within defined scope, time, and cost constraints.
Management effectiveness	In management, the ultimate measure of management's performance is the metric of management effectiveness which includes; execution, leadership, delegation, return on investment, conflict management, motivation, and consideration.
Profit	Profit refers to the return to the resource entrepreneurial ability; total revenue minus total cost.
Management information system	A computer-based system that provides information and support for effective managerial decision makin is referred to as a management information system.
Competitiveness	Competitiveness usually refers to characteristics that permit a firm to compete effectively with other firms due to low cost or superior technology, perhaps internationally.
Trend	Trend refers to the long-term movement of an economic variable, such as its average rate of increase or decrease over enough years to encompass several business cycles.
Competitor	Other organizations in the same industry or type of business that provide a good or service to the same set of customers is referred to as a competitor.
Balance	In banking and accountancy, the outstanding balance is the amount of money owned, (or due), that remains in a deposit account (or a loan account) at a given date, after all past remittances, payments and withdrawal have been accounted for. It can be positive (then, in the balance sheet of a firm, it is an asset) or negative (a liability).
Competitive market	A market in which no buyer or seller has market power is called a competitive market.
Operation	A standardized method or technique that is performed repetitively, often on different materials resulting in different finished goods is called an operation.
Structural change	Changes in the relative importance of different areas of an economy over time, usually measured in terms of their share of output, employment, or total spending is structural change.
Consideration	Consideration in contract law, a basic requirement for an enforceable agreement under traditional contract principles, defined in this text as legal value, bargained for and given in exchange for an

Go to **Cram101.com** for the Practice Tests for this Chapter.

act or promise. In corporation law, cash or property contributed to a corporation in exchange for shares, or a promise to contribute such cash or property.

Distribution	Distribution in economics, the manner in which total output and income is distributed among individuals or factors.
Merrill Lynch	Merrill Lynch through its subsidiaries and affiliates, provides capital markets services, investment banking and advisory services, wealth management, asset management, insurance, banking and related products and services on a global basis. It is best known for its Global Private Client services and its strong sales force.
Supply	Supply is the aggregate amount of any material good that can be called into being at a certain price point; it comprises one half of the equation of supply and demand. In classical economic theory, a curve representing supply is one of the factors that produce price.
Fund	Independent accounting entity with a self-balancing set of accounts segregated for the purposes of carrying on specific activities is referred to as a fund.
Deed	A deed is a legal instrument used to grant a right. The deed is best known as the method of transferring title to real estate from one person to another.
Bezos	Bezos founded Amazon.com in 1994, and became one of the most prominent dot-com billionaire entrepreneurs. In 2004, he started a human spaceflight start-up company called Blue Origin.
Credit	Credit refers to a recording as positive in the balance of payments, any transaction that gives rise to a payment into the country, such as an export, the sale of an asset, or borrowing from abroad.
Purchasing	Purchasing refers to the function in a firm that searches for quality material resources, finds the best suppliers, and negotiates the best price for goods and services.
Boot	Boot is any type of personal property received in a real property transaction that is not like kind, such as cash, mortgage notes, a boat or stock. The exchanger pays taxes on the boot to the extent of recognized capital gain. In an exchange if any funds are not used in purchasing the replacement property, that also will be called boot.
Internal integration	The creation of a collective identity and way of working and living together within an organization is referred to as internal integration.
Agent	A person who makes economic decisions for another economic actor. A hired manager operates as an agent for a firm's owner.
Tangible	Having a physical existence is referred to as the tangible. Personal property other than real estate, such as cars, boats, stocks, or other assets.
Executive information system	A management information system designed to facilitate strategic decision making at the highest levels of management by providing executives with easy access to timely and relevant information is called executive information system.
Context	The effect of the background under which a message often takes on more and richer meaning is a context. Context is especially important in cross-cultural interactions because some cultures are said to be high context or low context.
Success factor	The term success factor refers to the characteristics necessary for high performance; knowledge, skills, abilities, behaviors.
Toshiba	Toshiba is a Japanese high technology electrical and electronics manufacturing firm, headquartered in Tokyo, Japan. It is the 7th largest integrated manufacturer of electric and electronic equipment in the world.
Marginal cost	Marginal cost refers to the increase in cost that accompanies a unit increase in output; the partial derivative of the cost function with respect to output.

Leverage	Leverage is using given resources in such a way that the potential positive or negative outcome is magnified. In finance, this generally refers to borrowing.
Federal Express	The company officially began operations on April 17, 1973, utilizing a network of 14 Dassault Falcon 20s which connected 25 U.S. cities. FedEx, the first cargo airline to use jet aircraft for its services, expanded greatly after the deregulation of the cargo airlines sector. Federal Express use of the hub-spoke distribution paradigm in air freight enabled it to become a world leader in its field.
Prototyping	An iterative approach to design in which a series of mock-ups or models are developed until the customer and the designer come to agreement as to the final design is called prototyping.
Market research	Market research is the process of systematic gathering, recording and analyzing of data about customers, competitors and the market. Market research can help create a business plan, launch a new product or service, fine tune existing products and services, expand into new markets etc. It can be used to determine which portion of the population will purchase the product/service, based on variables like age, gender, location and income level. It can be found out what market characteristics your target market has.
Product mix	The combination of product lines offered by a manufacturer is referred to as product mix.
Segmentation Strategy	Segmentation strategy is a pricing strategy of focusing your marketing efforts to one or two narrow market segments and tailoring your marketing mix to these specialized markets, you can better meet the needs of that target market.
Loyalty	Marketers tend to define customer loyalty as making repeat purchases. Some argue that it should be defined attitudinally as a strongly positive feeling about the brand.
Safeway	On April 18, 2005, Safeway began a 100 million dollar brand re-positioning campaign labeled "Ingredients for life". This was done in an attempt to differentiate itself from its competitors, and to increase brand involvement. Steve Burd described it as "branding the shopping experience".
Commodity	Could refer to any good, but in trade a commodity is usually a raw material or primary product that enters into international trade, such as metals or basic agricultural products.
Basket	A basket is an economic term for a group of several securities created for the purpose of simultaneous buying or selling. Baskets are frequently used for program trading.
Devise	In a will, a gift of real property is called a devise.
Management system	A management system is the framework of processes and procedures used to ensure that an organization can fulfill all tasks required to achieve its objectives.
Systems design	Systems design is the process or art of defining the hardware and software architecture, components, modules, interfaces, and data for a computer system to satisfy specified requirements.
Argument	The discussion by counsel for the respective parties of their contentions on the law and the facts of the case being tried in order to aid the jury in arriving at a correct and just conclusion is called argument.
Marketing strategy	Marketing strategy refers to the means by which a marketing goal is to be achieved, usually characterized by a specified target market and a marketing program to reach it.
Derivative	A derivative is a generic term for specific types of investments from which payoffs over time are derived from the performance of assets (such as commodities, shares or bonds), interest rates, exchange rates, or indices (such as a stock market index, consumer price index (CPI) or an index of weather conditions).
Business operations	Business operations are those activities involved in the running of a business for the purpose of producing value for the stakeholders. The outcome of business operations is the harvesting of value from assets owned by a business.

Go to **Cram101.com** for the Practice Tests for this Chapter.

Boston Consulting Group	The Boston Consulting Group is a management consulting firm founded by Harvard Business School alum Bruce Henderson in 1963. In 1965 Bruce Henderson thought that to survive, much less grow, in a competitive landscape occupied by hundreds of larger and better-known consulting firms, a distinctive identity was needed, and pioneered "Business Strategy" as a special area of expertise.
Alignment	Term that refers to optimal coordination among disparate departments and divisions within a firm is referred to as alignment.
Business value	Business value is an informal term that includes all forms of value that determine the health and well-being of the firm in the long-run.
Strategic choice	Strategic choice refers to an organization's strategy; the ways an organization will attempt to fulfill its mission and achieve its long-term goals.
Strategy formulation	The process of deciding on a strategic direction by defining a company's mission and goals, its external opportunities and threats, and its internal strengths and weaknesses is referred to as a strategy formulation.
Instrument	Instrument refers to an economic variable that is controlled by policy makers and can be used to influence other variables, called targets. Examples are monetary and fiscal policies used to achieve external and internal balance.
Core	A core is the set of feasible allocations in an economy that cannot be improved upon by subset of the set of the economy's consumers (a coalition). In construction, when the force in an element is within a certain center section, the core, the element will only be under compression.
Regulation	Regulation refers to restrictions state and federal laws place on business with regard to the conduct of its activities.
Centralization	A structural policy in which decision-making authority is concentrated at the top of the organizational hierarchy is referred to as centralization.
Diffusion	Diffusion is the process by which a new idea or new product is accepted by the market. The rate of diffusion is the speed that the new idea spreads from one consumer to the next.
Organization culture	The set of values that helps the organization's employees understand which actions are considered acceptable and which unacceptable is referred to as the organization culture.
Optimum	Optimum refers to the best. Usually refers to a most preferred choice by consumers subject to a budget constraint or a profit maximizing choice by firms or industry subject to a technological constraint.
Process innovations	Innovations introducing into operations new and better ways of doing things are called process innovations. Nominations in this category must have made significant achievements in reducing environmental impacts of manufacturing processes, including the acquisition and refinement of materials used by the transportation industries in their products
Process innovation	The development and use of new or improved production or distribution methods is called process innovation. It is an approach in business process reengineering by which radical changes are made through innovations.
Virtual team	A group of physically dispersed people who work as a team via alternative communication modes is called virtual team.
Corporation	A legal entity chartered by a state or the Federal government that is distinct and separate from the individuals who own it is a corporation. This separation gives the corporation unique powers which other legal entities lack.
Patent	The legal right to the proceeds from and control over the use of an invented product or process, granted for a fixed period of time, usually 20 years. Patent is one form of intellectual property that is subject of the TRIPS agreement.

Go to **Cram101.com** for the Practice Tests for this Chapter.

Customer service	The ability of logistics management to satisfy users in terms of time, dependability, communication, and convenience is called the customer service.
Capital	Capital generally refers to financial wealth, especially that used to start or maintain a business. In classical economics, capital is one of four factors of production, the others being land and labor and entrepreneurship.
International trade	The export of goods and services from a country and the import of goods and services into a country is referred to as the international trade.
Harvard Business Review	Harvard Business Review is a research-based magazine written for business practitioners, it claims a high ranking business readership and enjoys the reverence of academics, executives, and management consultants. It has been the frequent publishing home for well known scholars and management thinkers.
Partnership	In the common law, a partnership is a type of business entity in which partners share with each other the profits or losses of the business undertaking in which they have all invested.
Market value	Market value refers to the price of an asset agreed on between a willing buyer and a willing seller; the price an asset could demand if it is sold on the open market.
Mistake	In contract law a mistake is incorrect understanding by one or more parties to a contract and may be used as grounds to invalidate the agreement. Common law has identified three different types of mistake in contract: unilateral mistake, mutual mistake, and common mistake.
Journal	Book of original entry, in which transactions are recorded in a general ledger system, is referred to as a journal.
Infomediaries	Intermdiaries in channels of distribution that specialize in the capture, analysis, application, and distribution of information are referred to as infomediaries.
Net worth	Net worth is the total assets minus total liabilities of an individual or company
Management science	Management science is the discipline of using mathematics, and other analytical methods, to help make better business decisions.
B2B marketplace	An electronic marketplace set up by an intermediary where buyers and sellers meet is a B2B marketplace.
Product life cycle	Product life cycle refers to a series of phases in a product's sales and cash flows over time; these phases, in order of occurrence, are introductory, growth, maturity, and decline.
Information technology management	Information technology management is a common business function within corporations. Strictly speaking, there are two incarnations to this definition. One implies the management of a collection of systems, infrastructure, and information that resides on them. Another implies the management of information technologies as a business function.
End user	End user refers to the ultimate user of a product or service.
Drucker	Drucker as a business thinker took off in the 1940s, when his initial writings on politics and society won him access to the internal workings of General Motors, which was one of the largest companies in the world at that time. His experiences in Europe had left him fascinated with the problem of authority.

20

Go to **Cram101.com** for the Practice Tests for this Chapter.

Consultant	A professional that provides expert advice in a particular field or area in which customers occassionaly require this type of knowledge is a consultant.
Competitive advantage	A business is said to have a competitive advantage when its unique strengths, often based on cost, quality, time, and innovation, offer consumers a greater percieved value and there by differtiating it from its competitors.
Competitor	Other organizations in the same industry or type of business that provide a good or service to the same set of customers is referred to as a competitor.
Management	Management characterizes the process of leading and directing all or part of an organization, often a business, through the deployment and manipulation of resources. Early twentieth-century management writer Mary Parker Follett defined management as "the art of getting things done through people."
Journal	Book of original entry, in which transactions are recorded in a general ledger system, is referred to as a journal.
Information system	An information system is a system whether automated or manual, that comprises people, machines, and/or methods organized to collect, process, transmit, and disseminate data that represent user information.
Strategic management	A philosophy of management that links strategic planning with dayto-day decision making. Strategic management seeks a fit between an organization's external and internal environments.
Technology	The body of knowledge and techniques that can be used to combine economic resources to produce goods and services is called technology.
Information technology	Information technology refers to technology that helps companies change business by allowing them to use new methods.
Competitiveness	Competitiveness usually refers to characteristics that permit a firm to compete effectively with other firms due to low cost or superior technology, perhaps internationally.
Asset	An item of property, such as land, capital, money, a share in ownership, or a claim on others for future payment, such as a bond or a bank deposit is an asset.
Firm	An organization that employs resources to produce a good or service for profit and owns and operates one or more plants is referred to as a firm.
Enabling	Enabling refers to giving workers the education and tools they need to assume their new decision-making powers.
Gain	In finance, gain is a profit or an increase in value of an investment such as a stock or bond. Gain is calculated by fair market value or the proceeds from the sale of the investment minus the sum of the purchase price and all costs associated with it.
Strategic planning	The process of determining the major goals of the organization and the policies and strategies for obtaining and using resources to achieve those goals is called strategic planning.
Business strategy	Business strategy, which refers to the aggregated operational strategies of single business firm or that of an SBU in a diversified corporation refers to the way in which a firm competes in its chosen arenas.
Maturity	Maturity refers to the final payment date of a loan or other financial instrument, after which point no further interest or principal need be paid.
Core	A core is the set of feasible allocations in an economy that cannot be improved upon by subset of the set of the economy's consumers (a coalition). In construction, when the force

Go to **Cram101.com** for the Practice Tests for this Chapter.

	in an element is within a certain center section, the core, the element will only be under compression.
Cash flow	In finance, cash flow refers to the amounts of cash being received and spent by a business during a defined period of time, sometimes tied to a specific project. Most of the time they are being used to determine gaps in the liquid position of a company.
Budget	Budget refers to an account, usually for a year, of the planned expenditures and the expected receipts of an entity. For a government, the receipts are tax revenues.
Planning horizon	The length of time it takes to conceive, develop, and complete a project and to recover the cost of the project on a discounted cash flow basis is referred to as planning horizon.
Market research	Market research is the process of systematic gathering, recording and analyzing of data about customers, competitors and the market. Market research can help create a business plan, launch a new product or service, fine tune existing products and services, expand into new markets etc. It can be used to determine which portion of the population will purchase the product/service, based on variables like age, gender, location and income level. It can be found out what market characteristics your target market has.
Market	A market is, as defined in economics, a social arrangement that allows buyers and sellers to discover information and carry out a voluntary exchange of goods or services.
Trend	Trend refers to the long-term movement of an economic variable, such as its average rate of increase or decrease over enough years to encompass several business cycles.
Future value	Future value measures what money is worth at a specified time in the future assuming a certain interest rate. This is used in time value of money calculations.
Value system	A value system refers to how an individual or a group of individuals organize their ethical or ideological values. A well-defined value system is a moral code.
Expense	In accounting, an expense represents an event in which an asset is used up or a liability is incurred. In terms of the accounting equation, expenses reduce owners' equity.
Balance	In banking and accountancy, the outstanding balance is the amount of money owned, (or due), that remains in a deposit account (or a loan account) at a given date, after all past remittances, payments and withdrawal have been accounted for. It can be positive (then, in the balance sheet of a firm, it is an asset) or negative (a liability).
Gap	In December of 1995, Gap became the first major North American retailer to accept independent monitoring of the working conditions in a contract factory producing its garments. Gap is the largest specialty retailer in the United States.
Portfolio	In finance, a portfolio is a collection of investments held by an institution or a private individual. Holding but not always a portfolio is part of an investment and risk-limiting strategy called diversification. By owning several assets, certain types of risk (in particular specific risk) can be reduced.
Unit cost	Unit cost refers to cost computed by dividing some amount of total costs by the related number of units. Also called average cost.
Service	Service refers to a "non tangible product" that is not embodied in a physical good and that typically effects some change in another product, person, or institution. Contrasts with good.
Innovation	Innovation refers to the first commercially successful introduction of a new product, the use of a new method of production, or the creation of a new form of business organization.
Industry	A group of firms that produce identical or similar products is an industry. It is also used specifically to refer to an area of economic production focused on manufacturing which

Go to **Cram101.com** for the Practice Tests for this Chapter.

	involves large amounts of capital investment before any profit can be realized, also called "heavy industry".
Creative strategy	A determination of what an advertising message will say or communicate to a target audience is called creative strategy.
Profit	Profit refers to the return to the resource entrepreneurial ability; total revenue minus total cost.
Context	The effect of the background under which a message often takes on more and richer meaning is a context. Context is especially important in cross-cultural interactions because some cultures are said to be high context or low context.
Strategy formulation	The process of deciding on a strategic direction by defining a company's mission and goals, its external opportunities and threats, and its internal strengths and weaknesses is referred to as a strategy formulation.
Project plan	A project plan lists the amount of time and the budget needed to complete the tasks involved in a project.
Privatization	A process in which investment bankers take companies that were previously owned by the government to the public markets is referred to as privatization.
Policy	Similar to a script in that a policy can be a less than completely rational decision-making method. Involves the use of a pre-existing set of decision steps for any problem that presents itself.
Financial measure	A financial measure is often used as a very simple mechanism to describe the performance of a business or investment. Because they are easily calculated they can not only be used to compare year on year results but also to compare and set norms for a particular type of business or investment.
Time horizon	A time horizon is a fixed point of time in the future at which point certain processes will be evaluated or assumed to end. It is necessary in an accounting, finance or risk management regime to assign such a fixed horizon time so that alternatives can be evaluated for performance over the same period of time.
Economic growth	Economic growth refers to the increase over time in the capacity of an economy to produce goods and services and to improve the well-being of its citizens.
Globalization	The increasing world-wide integration of markets for goods, services and capital that attracted special attention in the late 1990s is called globalization.
Household	An economic unit that provides the economy with resources and uses the income received to purchase goods and services that satisfy economic wants is called household.
Sears	Before the Sears catalog, farmers typically bought supplies (often at very high prices) from local general stores. Sears took advantage of this by publishing his catalog with clearly stated prices, so that consumers could know what he was selling and at what price, and order and obtain them conveniently. The catalog business soon grew quickly.
Shareholder	A shareholder is an individual or company (including a corporation) that legally owns one or more shares of stock in a joined stock company.
Brand	A name, symbol, or design that identifies the goods or services of one seller or group of sellers and distinguishes them from the goods and services of competitors is a brand.
Economy	The income, expenditures, and resources that affect the cost of running a business and household are called an economy.
Positioning	The art and science of fitting the product or service to one or more segments of the market

	in such a way as to set it meaningfully apart from competition is called positioning.
Enterprise	Enterprise refers to another name for a business organization. Other similar terms are business firm, sometimes simply business, sometimes simply firm, as well as company, and entity.
Comprehensive	A comprehensive refers to a layout accurate in size, color, scheme, and other necessary details to show how a final ad will look. For presentation only, never for reproduction.
Stakeholder	A stakeholder is an individual or group with a vested interest in or expectation for organizational performance. Usually stakeholders can either have an effect on or are affected by an organization.
Argument	The discussion by counsel for the respective parties of their contentions on the law and the facts of the case being tried in order to aid the jury in arriving at a correct and just conclusion is called argument.
Business opportunity	A business opportunity involves the sale or lease of any product, service, equipment, etc. that will enable the purchaser-licensee to begin a business
Free market	A free market is a market where price is determined by the unregulated interchange of supply and demand rather than set by artificial means.
Monetarism	Monetarism is a set of views concerning the determination of national income and monetary economics. It focuses on the supply and demand for money as the primary means by which economic activity is regulated.
Economics	The social science dealing with the use of scarce resources to obtain the maximum satisfaction of society's virtually unlimited economic wants is an economics.
Protectionism	Protectionism refers to advocacy of protection. The word has a negative connotation, and few advocates of protection in particular situations will acknowledge being protectionists.
Inflation rate	The percentage increase in the price level per year is an inflation rate. Alternatively, the inflation rate is the rate of decrease in the purchasing power of money.
Money market	The money market, in macroeconomics and international finance, refers to the equilibration of demand for a country's domestic money to its money supply; market for short-term financial instruments.
Inflation	An increase in the overall price level of an economy, usually as measured by the CPI or by the implicit price deflator is called inflation.
Commercializ-tion	Promoting a product to distributors and retailers to get wide distribution and developing strong advertising and sales campaigns to generate and maintain interest in the product among distributors and consumers is commercialization.
Restructuring	Restructuring is the corporate management term for the act of partially dismantling and reorganizing a company for the purpose of making it more efficient and therefore more profitable.
New economy	New economy, this term was used in the late 1990's to suggest that globalization and/or innovations in information technology had changed the way that the world economy works.
Investment	Investment refers to spending for the production and accumulation of capital and additions to inventories. In a financial sense, buying an asset with the expectation of making a return.
Option	A contract that gives the purchaser the option to buy or sell the underlying financial instrument at a specified price, called the exercise price or strike price, within a specific period of time.
Stock	In financial terminology, stock is the capital raized by a corporation, through the issuance

Go to **Cram101.com** for the Practice Tests for this Chapter.

and sale of shares.

Operation	A standardized method or technique that is performed repetitively, often on different materials resulting in different finished goods is called an operation.
Pension	A pension is a steady income given to a person (usually after retirement). Pensions are typically payments made in the form of a guaranteed annuity to a retired or disabled employee.
Channel of communication	The means of conveying a message to a receiver is channel of communication.
Channel	Channel, in communications (sometimes called communications channel), refers to the medium used to convey information from a sender (or transmitter) to a receiver.
Social responsibility	Social responsibility is a doctrine that claims that an entity whether it is state, government, corporation, organization or individual has a responsibility to society.
Maastricht Treaty	Treaty agreed to in 1991, but not ratified until January 1, 1994, that committed the 12 member states of the European Community to a closer economic and political union is the Maastricht Treaty.
Trade barrier	An artificial disincentive to export and/or import, such as a tariff, quota, or other NTB is called a trade barrier.
Forming	The first stage of team development, where the team is formed and the objectives for the team are set is referred to as forming.
Union	A worker association that bargains with employers over wages and working conditions is called a union.
Buying power	The dollar amount available to purchase securities on margin is buying power. The amount is calculated by adding the cash held in the brokerage accounts and the amount that could be spent if securities were fully margined to their limit. If an investor uses their buying power, they are purchasing securities on credit.
Domestic	From or in one's own country. A domestic producer is one that produces inside the home country. A domestic price is the price inside the home country. Opposite of 'foreign' or 'world.'.
Corporation	A legal entity chartered by a state or the Federal government that is distinct and separate from the individuals who own it is a corporation. This separation gives the corporation unique powers which other legal entities lack.
Interest	In finance and economics, interest is the price paid by a borrower for the use of a lender's money. In other words, interest is the amount of paid to "rent" money for a period of time.
Consumption	In Keynesian economics consumption refers to personal consumption expenditure, i.e., the purchase of currently produced goods and services out of income, out of savings (net worth), or from borrowed funds. It refers to that part of disposable income that does not go to saving.
Advertising	Advertising refers to paid, nonpersonal communication through various media by organizations and individuals who are in some way identified in the advertising message.
Disclosure	Disclosure means the giving out of information, either voluntarily or to be in compliance with legal regulations or workplace rules.
Purchasing	Purchasing refers to the function in a firm that searches for quality material resources, finds the best suppliers, and negotiates the best price for goods and services.
Intellectual	In law, intellectual property is an umbrella term for various legal entitlements which

Go to **Cram101.com** for the Practice Tests for this Chapter.

property	attach to certain types of information, ideas, or other intangibles in their expressed form. The holder of this legal entitlement is generally entitled to exercise various exclusive rights in relation to its subject matter.
Royalties	Remuneration paid to the owners of technology, patents, or trade names for the use of same name are called royalties.
Property	Assets defined in the broadest legal sense. Property includes the unrealized receivables of a cash basis taxpayer, but not services rendered.
Fraud	Tax fraud falls into two categories: civil and criminal. Under civil fraud, the IRS may impose as a penalty of an amount equal to as much as 75 percent of the underpayment.
Scope	Scope of a project is the sum total of all projects products and their requirements or features.
World Trade Organization	The World Trade Organization is an international, multilateral organization, which sets the rules for the global trading system and resolves disputes between its member states, all of whom are signatories to its approximately 30 agreements.
Research and development	The use of resources for the deliberate discovery of new information and ways of doing things, together with the application of that information in inventing new products or processes is referred to as research and development.
Misuse	A defense that relieves a seller of product liability if the user abnormally misused the product is called misuse. Products must be designed to protect against foreseeable misuse.
Buyer	A buyer refers to a role in the buying center with formal authority and responsibility to select the supplier and negotiate the terms of the contract.
Public sector	Public sector refers to the part of the economy that contains all government entities; government.
Exchange	The trade of things of value between buyer and seller so that each is better off after the trade is called the exchange.
Trade association	An industry trade group or trade association is generally a public relations organization founded and funded by corporations that operate in a specific industry. Its purpose is generally to promote that industry through PR activities such as advertizing, education, political donations, political pressure, publishing, and astroturfing.
Regulation	Regulation refers to restrictions state and federal laws place on business with regard to the conduct of its activities.
Protocol	Protocol refers to a statement that, before product development begins, identifies a well-defined target market; specific customers' needs, wants, and preferences; and what the product will be and do.
De facto	De facto, in fact, actual. Often used in contrast to de jure to refer to a real state of affairs.
Boom and bust	In economics, the term boom and bust refers to the movement of an economy through economic cycles due to changes in aggregate demand. During booms, there is a high level of aggregate demand, inflation increases, unemployment falls, and growth in national income accelerates. During busts, or recessions, when aggregate demand is low, inflation decreases, unemployment rises and national income falls.
Market price	Market price is an economic concept with commonplace familiarity; it is the price that a good or service is offered at, or will fetch, in the marketplace; it is of interest mainly in the study of microeconomics.

Dividend	Amount of corporate profits paid out for each share of stock is referred to as dividend.
Preference	The act of a debtor in paying or securing one or more of his creditors in a manner more favorable to them than to other creditors or to the exclusion of such other creditors is a preference. In the absence of statute, a preference is perfectly good, but to be legal it must be bona fide, and not a mere subterfuge of the debtor to secure a future benefit to himself or to prevent the application of his property to his debts.
Functional structure	A type of structure in which units and departments are organized based on the activity or function that they perform is called the functional structure.
Business unit	The lowest level of the company which contains the set of functions that carry a product through its life span from concept through manufacture, distribution, sales and service is a business unit.
Vision statement	The identification of objectives to be achieved in the future is called vision statement.
Situation analysis	Taking stock of where the fine or product has been recently, where it is now, and where it is headed in terms of the organization's plans and the external factors and trends affecting it is a situation analysis.
Brainstorming	Brainstorming refers to a technique designed to overcome our natural tendency to evaluate and criticize ideas and thereby reduce the creative output of those ideas. People are encouraged to produce ideas/options without criticizing, often at a very fast pace to minimize our natural tendency to criticize.
Scenario planning	Scenario planning or Scenario thinking is a strategic planning method that some organizations use to make flexible long-term plans. The basic method is that a group of analysts generate simulation games for policy makers.
Control activities	Control activities are the activities intended to prevent, detect, and correct errors and irregularities relating to business risks. Policies and procedures used by management to meet its objectives.
Performance measurement	The process by which someone evaluates an employee's work behaviors by measurement and comparison with previously established standards, documents the results, and communicates the results to the employee is called performance measurement.
Feedback loop	Feedback loop consists of a response and feedback. It is a system where outputs are fed back into the system as inputs, increasing or decreasing effects.
Complexity	The technical sophistication of the product and hence the amount of understanding required to use it is referred to as complexity. It is the opposite of simplicity.
Alignment	Term that refers to optimal coordination among disparate departments and divisions within a firm is referred to as alignment.
Product life cycle	Product life cycle refers to a series of phases in a product's sales and cash flows over time; these phases, in order of occurrence, are introductory, growth, maturity, and decline.
Market share	That fraction of an industry's output accounted for by an individual firm or group of firms is called market share.
Economies of scale	In economics, returns to scale and economies of scale are related terms that describe what happens as the scale of production increases. They are different terms and not to be used interchangeably.
Experience curve	Experience curve refers to function that measures the decline in cost per unit in various value-chain functions such as manufacturing, marketing, distribution, and so on, as units produced increases.

Go to **Cram101.com** for the Practice Tests for this Chapter.

Manufacturing	Production of goods primarily by the application of labor and capital to raw materials and other intermediate inputs, in contrast to agriculture, mining, forestry, fishing, and services a manufacturing.
Production	The creation of finished goods and services using the factors of production: land, labor, capital, entrepreneurship, and knowledge.
Relative market share	Relative market share refers to the sales of a firm or SBU divided by the sales of the largest firm in the industry; often used as the horizontal axis in business portfolio analysis.
Market position	Market position is a measure of the position of a company or product on a market.
Premium	Premium refers to the fee charged by an insurance company for an insurance policy. The rate of losses must be relatively predictable: In order to set the premium (prices) insurers must be able to estimate them accurately.
Supply	Supply is the aggregate amount of any material good that can be called into being at a certain price point; it comprises one half of the equation of supply and demand. In classical economic theory, a curve representing supply is one of the factors that produce price.
Product cost	Product cost refers to sum of the costs assigned to a product for a specific purpose. A concept used in applying the cost plus approach to product pricing in which only the costs of manufacturing the product are included in the cost amount to which the markup is added.
Distribution channel	A distribution channel is a chain of intermediaries, each passing a product down the chain to the next organization, before it finally reaches the consumer or end-user.
Administrative cost	An administrative cost is all executive, organizational, and clerical costs associated with the general management of an organization rather than with manufacturing, marketing, or selling
Inventory control	Inventory control, in the field of loss prevention, are systems designed to introduce technical barriers to shoplifting.
Sales forecasting	Sales forecasting refers to the process of predicting sales of services or goods. The initial step in preparing a master budget.
Customer database	Customer database refers to a computer database specifically designed for storage, retrieval, and analysis of customer data by marketers.
Customer service	The ability of logistics management to satisfy users in terms of time, dependability, communication, and convenience is called the customer service.
Finished goods	Completed products awaiting sale are called finished goods. An item considered a finished good in a supplying plant might be considered a component or raw material in a receiving plant.
Contribution	In business organization law, the cash or property contributed to a business by its owners is referred to as contribution.
Distribution	Distribution in economics, the manner in which total output and income is distributed among individuals or factors.
Inventory	Tangible property held for sale in the normal course of business or used in producing goods or services for sale is an inventory.
Logistics	Those activities that focus on getting the right amount of the right products to the right place at the right time at the lowest possible cost is referred to as logistics.
Promotion	Promotion refers to all the techniques sellers use to motivate people to buy products or services. An attempt by marketers to inform people about products and to persuade them to

Go to **Cram101.com** for the Practice Tests for this Chapter.

participate in an exchange.

Margin	A deposit by a buyer in stocks with a seller or a stockbroker, as security to cover fluctuations in the market in reference to stocks that the buyer has purchased but for which he has not paid is a margin. Commodities are also traded on margin.
Users	Users refer to people in the organization who actually use the product or service purchased by the buying center.
Boston Consulting Group	The Boston Consulting Group is a management consulting firm founded by Harvard Business School alum Bruce Henderson in 1963. In 1965 Bruce Henderson thought that to survive, much less grow, in a competitive landscape occupied by hundreds of larger and better-known consulting firms, a distinctive identity was needed, and pioneered "Business Strategy" as a special area of expertise.
Revenue	Revenue is a U.S. business term for the amount of money that a company receives from its activities, mostly from sales of products and/or services to customers.
Cash cow	A cash cow is a product or a business unit that generates unusually high profit margins: so high that it is responsible for a large amount of a company's operating profit.
Rate of return	A rate of return is a comparison of the money earned (or lost) on an investment to the amount of money invested.
Market opportunities	Market opportunities refer to areas where a company believes there are favorable demand trends, needs, and/or wants that are not being satisfied, and where it can compete effectively.
Cash inflow	Cash coming into the company as the result of a previous investment is a cash inflow.
Industry attractiveness	Industry attractiveness refers to the relative industry profitability outlook for an industry in relation to the expected average profitability of all industry.
Variable	A variable is something measured by a number; it is used to analyze what happens to other things when the size of that number changes.
Shares	Shares refer to an equity security, representing a shareholder's ownership of a corporation. Shares are one of a finite number of equal portions in the capital of a company, entitling the owner to a proportion of distributed, non-reinvested profits known as dividends and to a portion of the value of the company in case of liquidation.
Brand image	The advertising metric that measures the type and favorability of consumer perceptions of the brand is referred to as the brand image.
Declining industry	An industry in which economic profits are negative and that will, therefore, decrease its output as firms leave it is called declining industry.
Matching	Matching refers to an accounting concept that establishes when expenses are recognized. Expenses are matched with the revenues they helped to generate and are recognized when those revenues are recognized.
Optimum	Optimum refers to the best. Usually refers to a most preferred choice by consumers subject to a budget constraint or a profit maximizing choice by firms or industry subject to a technological constraint.
Supply and demand	The partial equilibrium supply and demand economic model originally developed by Alfred Marshall attempts to describe, explain, and predict changes in the price and quantity of goods sold in competitive markets.
Capacity utilization	Capacity utilization is a concept in Economics which refers to the extent to which an enterprise or a nation actually uses its installed productive capacity. Thus, it refers to

Go to **Cram101.com** for the Practice Tests for this Chapter.

	the relationship between actual output produced and potential output that could be produced with installed equipment, if capacity was fully used.
Productivity	Productivity refers to the total output of goods and services in a given period of time divided by work hours.
Deliverable	A deliverable refers to a product created as a result of project work.
Niche market	A niche market or market niche is a focused, targetable portion of a market. By definition, then, a business that focuses on a niche market is addressing a need for a product or service that is not being addressed by mainstream providers.
Niche	In industry, a niche is a situation or an activity perfectly suited to a person. A niche can imply a working position or an area suited to a person who occupies it. Basically, a job where a person is able to succeed and thrive.
Integration	Economic integration refers to reducing barriers among countries to transactions and to movements of goods, capital, and labor, including harmonization of laws, regulations, and standards. Integrated markets theoretically function as a unified market.
Diversification	Investing in a collection of assets whose returns do not always move together, with the result that overall risk is lower than for individual assets is referred to as diversification.
Acquisition	A company's purchase of the property and obligations of another company is an acquisition.
Competitive Strategy	An outline of how a business intends to compete with other firms in the same industry is called competitive strategy.
Retailing	All activities involved in selling, renting, and providing goods and services to ultimate consumers for personal, family, or household use is referred to as retailing.
Substitute product	Any product viewed by a consumer as an alternative for other products is a substitute product. The substitution is rarely perfect, and varies from time to time depending on price, availability, etc.
Advertising campaign	A comprehensive advertising plan that consists of a series of messages in a variety of media that center on a single theme or idea is referred to as an advertising campaign.
Price war	Price war refers to successive and continued decreases in the prices charged by firms in an oligopolistic industry. Each firm lowers its price below rivals' prices, hoping to increase its sales and revenues at its rivals' expense.
Switching costs	Switching costs is a term used in microeconomics, strategic management, and marketing to describe any impediment to a customer's changing of suppliers. In many markets, consumers are forced to incur costs when switching from one supplier to another. These costs are called switching costs and can come in many different shapes.
Entry barrier	An entry barrier or barrier to entry is an obstacle in the path of a potential firm which wants to enter a given market.
Loyalty	Marketers tend to define customer loyalty as making repeat purchases. Some argue that it should be defined attitudinally as a strongly positive feeling about the brand.
Fixed cost	The cost that a firm bears if it does not produce at all and that is independent of its output. The presence of a fixed cost tends to imply increasing returns to scale. Contrasts with variable cost.
Commodity	Could refer to any good, but in trade a commodity is usually a raw material or primary product that enters into international trade, such as metals or basic agricultural products.
Backward	A form of vertical integration that involves the purchase of suppliers in order to reduce

integration	dependency is backward integration.
Forward integration	Practice in corporate vertical marketing system in which a producer also owns retail shops is a forward integration.
Flexible manufacturing	Flexible manufacturing refers to designing machines to do multiple tasks so that they can produce a variety of products.
Price competition	Price competition is where a company tries to distinguish its product or service from competing products on the basis of low price.
Parallel development	An approach to new product development that involves cross-functional team members who conduct the simultaneous development of both the product and the production process, staying with the product from conception to production is a parallel development.
Security	Security refers to a claim on the borrower future income that is sold by the borrower to the lender. A security is a type of transferable interest representing financial value.
Reuters	Reuters is best known as a news service that provides reports from around the world to newspapers and broadcasters. Its main focus is on supplying the financial markets with information and trading products.
Broker	In commerce, a broker is a party that mediates between a buyer and a seller. A broker who also acts as a seller or as a buyer becomes a principal party to the deal.
Target market	One or more specific groups of potential consumers toward which an organization directs its marketing program are a target market.
Insurance	Insurance refers to a system by which individuals can reduce their exposure to risk of large losses by spreading the risks among a large number of persons.
Recruitment	Recruitment refers to the set of activities used to obtain a sufficient number of the right people at the right time; its purpose is to select those who best meet the needs of the organization.
Advertisement	Advertisement is the promotion of goods, services, companies and ideas, usually by an identified sponsor. Marketers see advertising as part of an overall promotional strategy.
Cost advantage	Possession of a lower cost of production or operation than a competing firm or country is cost advantage.
Configuration	An organization's shape, which reflects the division of labor and the means of coordinating the divided tasks is configuration.
Auction	A preexisting business model that operates successfully on the Internet by announcing an item for sale and permitting multiple purchasers to bid on them under specified rules and condition is an auction.
Specialist	A specialist is a trader who makes a market in one or several stocks and holds the limit order book for those stocks.
Stock exchange	A stock exchange is a corporation or mutual organization which provides facilities for stock brokers and traders, to trade company stocks and other securities.
Derivative	A derivative is a generic term for specific types of investments from which payoffs over time are derived from the performance of assets (such as commodities, shares or bonds), interest rates, exchange rates, or indices (such as a stock market index, consumer price index (CPI) or an index of weather conditions).
Futures	Futures refer to contracts for the sale and future delivery of stocks or commodities, wherein either party may waive delivery, and receive or pay, as the case may be, the difference in market price at the time set for delivery.

Go to **Cram101.com** for the Practice Tests for this Chapter.

Merger	Merger refers to the combination of two firms into a single firm.
Wholesaling	Wholesaling consists of the sale of goods/merchandise to retailers, to industrial, commercial, institutional, or other professional business users or to other wholesalers and related subordinated services.
Warehouse	Warehouse refers to a location, often decentralized, that a firm uses to store, consolidate, age, or mix stock; house product-recall programs; or ease tax burdens.
Consignment	Consignment refers to a bailment for sale. The consignee does not undertake the absolute obligation to sell or pay for the goods.
Automation	Automation allows machines to do work previously accomplished by people.
Workflow	Workflow refers to automated systems that electronically route documents to the next person in the process.
Yield	The interest rate that equates a future value or an annuity to a given present value is a yield.
Barriers to entry	In economics and especially in the theory of competition, barriers to entry are obstacles in the path of a firm which wants to enter a given market.
Point of Sale	Point of sale can mean a retail shop, a checkout counter in a shop, or a variable location where a transaction occurs.
Supply chain	Supply chain refers to the flow of goods, services, and information from the initial sources of materials and services to the delivery of products to consumers.
Product mix	The combination of product lines offered by a manufacturer is referred to as product mix.
Leverage	Leverage is using given resources in such a way that the potential positive or negative outcome is magnified. In finance, this generally refers to borrowing.
Layout	Layout refers to the physical arrangement of the various parts of an advertisement including the headline, subheads, illustrations, body copy, and any identifying marks.
Disintermediation	A reduction in the flow of funds into the banking system that causes the amount financial intermediation to decline is referred to as disintermediation.
Reintermediation	Reintermediation can be defined as the reintroduction of an intermediary between end users (consumers) and a producer.
Intermediaries	Intermediaries specialize in information either to bring together two parties to a transaction or to buy in order to sell again.
Value chain	The sequence of business functions in which usefulness is added to the products or services of a company is a value chain.
Customer loyalty	Marketers tend to define customer loyalty as making repeat purchases. Some argue that it should be defined attitudinally as a strongly positive feeling about the brand.
Market segments	Market segments refer to the groups that result from the process of market segmentation; these groups ideally have common needs and will respond similarly to a marketing action.
Quality control	The measurement of products and services against set standards is referred to as quality control.
Variance	Variance refers to a measure of how much an economic or statistical variable varies across values or observations. Its calculation is the same as that of the covariance, being the covariance of the variable with itself.
Dealer	People who link buyers with sellers by buying and selling securities at stated prices are

referred to as a dealer.

Agent	A person who makes economic decisions for another economic actor. A hired manager operates as an agent for a firm's owner.
Electronic commerce	Electronic commerce or e-commerce, refers to any activity that uses some form of electronic communication in the inventory, exchange, advertisement, distribution, and payment of goods and services.
Commerce	Commerce is the exchange of something of value between two entities. It is the central mechanism from which capitalism is derived.
Invoice	The itemized bill for a transaction, stating the nature of the transaction and its cost. In international trade, the invoice price is often the preferred basis for levying an ad valorem tariff.
Relative cost	Relative cost refers to the relationship between the price paid for advertising time or space and the size of the audience delivered; it is used to compare the prices of various media vehicles.
Fund	Independent accounting entity with a self-balancing set of accounts segregated for the purposes of carrying on specific activities is referred to as a fund.
Differentiation Strategy	Differentiation strategy requires innovation and significant points of difference in product offerings, brand image, higher quality, advanced technology, or superior service in a relatively broad array of market segments.
Cost leadership	Organization's ability to achieve lower costs relative to competitors through productivity and efficiency improvements, elimination of waste, and tight cost control is cost leadership.
Leadership	Management merely consists of leadership applied to business situations; or in other words: management forms a sub-set of the broader process of leadership.
Management control	That aspect of management concerned with the comparison of actual versus planned performance as well as the development and implementation of procedures to correct substandard performance is called management control.
Corporate image	A corporate image refers to how a corporation is perceived. It is a generally accepted image of what a company "stands for".
Sales analysis	A tool for controlling marketing programs using sales records to compare actual results with sales goals and to identify strengths and weaknesses is called sales analysis.
Small business	Small business refers to a business that is independently owned and operated, is not dominant in its field of operation, and meets certain standards of size in terms of employees or annual receipts.
Business process	Business process refers to the individual activities of an enterprise. Processes can be viewed at a high level, for example, 'marketing,' or at the level of detailed subprocesses, for example, 'customer retention.'.
Data warehouse	A Data warehouse is a repository of integrated information, available for queries and analysis. Data and information are extracted from heterogeneous sources as they are generated.
Market niche	A market niche or niche market is a focused, targetable portion of a market. By definition, then, a business that focuses on a niche market is addressing a need for a product or service that is not being addressed by mainstream providers.
Mortgage	Mortgage refers to a note payable issued for property, such as a house, usually repaid in equal installments consisting of part principle and part interest, over a specified period.

Estate	An estate is the totality of the legal rights, interests, entitlements and obligations attaching to property. In the context of wills and probate, it refers to the totality of the property which the deceased owned or in which some interest was held.
Customer value	Customer value refers to the unique combination of benefits received by targeted buyers that includes quality, price, convenience, on-time delivery, and both before-sale and after-sale service.
Consideration	Consideration in contract law, a basic requirement for an enforceable agreement under traditional contract principles, defined in this text as legal value, bargained for and given in exchange for an act or promise. In corporation law, cash or property contributed to a corporation in exchange for shares, or a promise to contribute such cash or property.
Procurement	Procurement is the acquisition of goods or services at the best possible total cost of ownership, in the right quantity, at the right time, in the right place for the direct benefit or use of the governments, corporations, or individuals generally via, but not limited to a contract.
Assessment	Collecting information and providing feedback to employees about their behavior, communication style, or skills is an assessment.
Discount	The difference between the face value of a bond and its selling price, when a bond is sold for less than its face value it's referred to as a discount.
Holding	The holding is a court's determination of a matter of law based on the issue presented in the particular case. In other words: under this law, with these facts, this result.
Customer satisfaction	Customer satisfaction is a business term which is used to capture the idea of measuring how satisfied an enterprise's customers are with the organization's efforts in a marketplace.
Product innovation	The development and sale of a new or improved product is a product innovation. Production of a new product on a commercial basis.
Instrument	Instrument refers to an economic variable that is controlled by policy makers and can be used to influence other variables, called targets. Examples are monetary and fiscal policies used to achieve external and internal balance.
Assimilation	Assimilation refers to the process through which a minority group learns the ways of the dominant group. In organizations, this means that when people of different types and backgrounds are hired, the organization attempts to mold them to fit the existing organizational culture.
Senior management	Senior management is generally a team of individuals at the highest level of organizational management who have the day-to-day responsibilities of managing a corporation.

Strategic management	A philosophy of management that links strategic planning with dayto-day decision making. Strategic management seeks a fit between an organization's external and internal environments.
Management	Management characterizes the process of leading and directing all or part of an organization, often a business, through the deployment and manipulation of resources. Early twentieth-century management writer Mary Parker Follett defined management as "the art of getting things done through people."
Journal	Book of original entry, in which transactions are recorded in a general ledger system, is referred to as a journal.
Stock	In financial terminology, stock is the capital raized by a corporation, through the issuance and sale of shares.
Harvard Business Review	Harvard Business Review is a research-based magazine written for business practitioners, it claims a high ranking business readership and enjoys the reverence of academics, executives, and management consultants. It has been the frequent publishing home for well known scholars and management thinkers.
Social responsibility	Social responsibility is a doctrine that claims that an entity whether it is state, government, corporation, organization or individual has a responsibility to society.
Competitive Strategy	An outline of how a business intends to compete with other firms in the same industry is called competitive strategy.
Strategic planning	The process of determining the major goals of the organization and the policies and strategies for obtaining and using resources to achieve those goals is called strategic planning.
New economy	New economy, this term was used in the late 1990's to suggest that globalization and/or innovations in information technology had changed the way that the world economy works.
Competitor	Other organizations in the same industry or type of business that provide a good or service to the same set of customers is referred to as a competitor.
Industry	A group of firms that produce identical or similar products is an industry. It is also used specifically to refer to an area of economic production focused on manufacturing which involves large amounts of capital investment before any profit can be realized, also called "heavy industry".
Economy	The income, expenditures, and resources that affect the cost of running a business and household are called an economy.
Marketing	Promoting and selling products or services to customers, or prospective customers, is referred to as marketing.
Strategy formulation	The process of deciding on a strategic direction by defining a company's mission and goals, its external opportunities and threats, and its internal strengths and weaknesses is referred to as a strategy formulation.
Corporate Strategy	Corporate strategy is concerned with the firm's choice of business, markets and activities and thus it defines the overall scope and direction of the business.
Management science	Management science is the discipline of using mathematics, and other analytical methods, to help make better business decisions.
Prentice Hall	Prentice Hall is a leading educational publisher. It is an imprint of the Pearson Education Company, based in New Jersey, USA.
Derivative	A derivative is a generic term for specific types of investments from which payoffs over time

Go to **Cram101.com** for the Practice Tests for this Chapter.

are derived from the performance of assets (such as commodities, shares or bonds), interest rates, exchange rates, or indices (such as a stock market index, consumer price index (CPI) or an index of weather conditions).

Exchange	The trade of things of value between buyer and seller so that each is better off after the trade is called the exchange.
Buyer	A buyer refers to a role in the buying center with formal authority and responsibility to select the supplier and negotiate the terms of the contract.
Firm	An organization that employs resources to produce a good or service for profit and owns and operates one or more plants is referred to as a firm.
Competitive advantage	A business is said to have a competitive advantage when its unique strengths, often based on cost, quality, time, and innovation, offer consumers a greater percieved value and there by diffetiating it from its competitors.
Information technology	Information technology refers to technology that helps companies change business by allowing them to use new methods.
Information system	An information system is a system whether automated or manual, that comprises people, machines, and/or methods organized to collect, process, transmit, and disseminate data that represent user information.
Market leader	The market leader is dominant in its industry. It has substantial market share and often extensive distribution arrangements with retailers. It typically is the industry leader in developing innovative new business models and new products (although not always).
HarperCollins	HarperCollins is a publishing organization owned by News Corporation. The company found success in 1841 as a printer of Bibles, and in 1848 Collins's son Sir William Collins developed the firm as a publishing venture, specializing in religious and educational books.
Technology	The body of knowledge and techniques that can be used to combine economic resources to produce goods and services is called technology.
Market	A market is, as defined in economics, a social arrangement that allows buyers and sellers to discover information and carry out a voluntary exchange of goods or services.
Business opportunity	A business opportunity involves the sale or lease of any product, service, equipment, etc. that will enable the purchaser-licensee to begin a business
Investment	Investment refers to spending for the production and accumulation of capital and additions to inventories. In a financial sense, buying an asset with the expectation of making a return.
Alignment	Term that refers to optimal coordination among disparate departments and divisions within a firm is referred to as alignment.
Continuous process	An uninterrupted production process in which long production runs turn out finished goods over time is called continuous process.
Business strategy	Business strategy, which refers to the aggregated operational strategies of single business firm or that of an SBU in a diversified corporation refers to the way in which a firm competes in its chosen arenas.
Deliverable	A deliverable refers to a product created as a result of project work.
Argument	The discussion by counsel for the respective parties of their contentions on the law and the facts of the case being tried in order to aid the jury in arriving at a correct and just conclusion is called argument.
Maturity	Maturity refers to the final payment date of a loan or other financial instrument, after which point no further interest or principal need be paid.

Portfolio	In finance, a portfolio is a collection of investments held by an institution or a private individual. Holding but not always a portfolio is part of an investment and risk-limiting strategy called diversification. By owning several assets, certain types of risk (in particular specific risk) can be reduced.
Senior management	Senior management is generally a team of individuals at the highest level of organizational management who have the day-to-day responsibilities of managing a corporation.
Users	Users refer to people in the organization who actually use the product or service purchased by the buying center.
Innovation	Innovation refers to the first commercially successful introduction of a new product, the use of a new method of production, or the creation of a new form of business organization.
Evaluation	The consumer's appraisal of the product or brand on important attributes is called evaluation.
Context	The effect of the background under which a message often takes on more and richer meaning is a context. Context is especially important in cross-cultural interactions because some cultures are said to be high context or low context.
Senior executive	Senior executive means a chief executive officer, chief operating officer, chief financial officer and anyone in charge of a principal business unit or function.
Specialist	A specialist is a trader who makes a market in one or several stocks and holds the limit order book for those stocks.
Coalition	An informal alliance among managers who support a specific goal is called coalition.
Complexity	The technical sophistication of the product and hence the amount of understanding required to use it is referred to as complexity. It is the opposite of simplicity.
Integration	Economic integration refers to reducing barriers among countries to transactions and to movements of goods, capital, and labor, including harmonization of laws, regulations, and standards. Integrated markets theoretically function as a unified market.
Consultant	A professional that provides expert advice in a particular field or area in which customers occassionaly require this type of knowledge is a consultant.
Expense budget	A budget that outlines the anticipated and actual expenses for each responsibility center is referred to as expense budget.
Expense	In accounting, an expense represents an event in which an asset is used up or a liability is incurred. In terms of the accounting equation, expenses reduce owners' equity.
Capital	Capital generally refers to financial wealth, especially that used to start or maintain a business. In classical economics, capital is one of four factors of production, the others being land and labor and entrepreneurship.
Budget	Budget refers to an account, usually for a year, of the planned expenditures and the expected receipts of an entity. For a government, the receipts are tax revenues.
Management team	A management team is directly responsible for managing the day-to-day operations (and profitability) of a company.
Diffusion	Diffusion is the process by which a new idea or new product is accepted by the market. The rate of diffusion is the speed that the new idea spreads from one consumer to the next.
Decentralization	Decentralization is the process of redistributing decision-making closer to the point of service or action. This gives freedom to managers at lower levels of the organization to make decisions.

Go to **Cram101.com** for the Practice Tests for this Chapter.

Utility	Utility refers to the want-satisfying power of a good or service; the satisfaction or pleasure a consumer obtains from the consumption of a good or service.
Strategic plan	The formal document that presents the ways and means by which a strategic goal will be achieved is a strategic plan. A long-term flexible plan that does not regulate activities but rather outlines the means to achieve certain results, and provides the means to alter the course of action should the desired ends change.
Credibility	The extent to which a source is perceived as having knowledge, skill, or experience relevant to a communication topic and can be trusted to give an unbiased opinion or present objective information on the issue is called credibility.
Gap	In December of 1995, Gap became the first major North American retailer to accept independent monitoring of the working conditions in a contract factory producing its garments. Gap is the largest specialty retailer in the United States.
Middle management	Middle management refers to the level of management that includes general managers, division managers, and branch and plant managers who are responsible for tactical planning and controlling.
Respondent	Respondent refers to a term often used to describe the party charged in an administrative proceeding. The party adverse to the appellant in a case appealed to a higher court.
Personnel	A collective term for all of the employees of an organization. Personnel is also commonly used to refer to the personnel management function or the organizational unit responsible for administering personnel programs.
Action plan	Action plan refers to a written document that includes the steps the trainee and manager will take to ensure that training transfers to the job.
Critical success factor	Critical Success Factor is a business term for an element which is necessary for an organization or project to achieve its mission.
Performance target	A task established for an employee that provides the comparative basis for performance appraisal is a performance target.
Mission statement	Mission statement refers to an outline of the fundamental purposes of an organization.
Success factor	The term success factor refers to the characteristics necessary for high performance; knowledge, skills, abilities, behaviors.
Option	A contract that gives the purchaser the option to buy or sell the underlying financial instrument at a specified price, called the exercise price or strike price, within a specific period of time.
Fund	Independent accounting entity with a self-balancing set of accounts segregated for the purposes of carrying on specific activities is referred to as a fund.
Comprehensive	A comprehensive refers to a layout accurate in size, color, scheme, and other necessary details to show how a final ad will look. For presentation only, never for reproduction.
Return on investment	Return on investment refers to the return a businessperson gets on the money he and other owners invest in the firm; for example, a business that earned $100 on a $1,000 investment would have a ROI of 10 percent: 100 divided by 1000.
Business value	Business value is an informal term that includes all forms of value that determine the health and well-being of the firm in the long-run.
American Airlines	American Airlines developed from a conglomeration of about 82 small airlines through a series of corporate acquisitions and reorganizations: initially, the name American Airways was used

	as a common brand by a number of independent air carriers. American Airlines is the largest airline in the world in terms of total passengers transported and fleet size, and the second-largest airline in the world.
Merrill Lynch	Merrill Lynch through its subsidiaries and affiliates, provides capital markets services, investment banking and advisory services, wealth management, asset management, insurance, banking and related products and services on a global basis. It is best known for its Global Private Client services and its strong sales force.
Supply	Supply is the aggregate amount of any material good that can be called into being at a certain price point; it comprises one half of the equation of supply and demand. In classical economic theory, a curve representing supply is one of the factors that produce price.
EBay	eBay manages an online auction and shopping website, where people buy and sell goods and services worldwide.
Customer service	The ability of logistics management to satisfy users in terms of time, dependability, communication, and convenience is called the customer service.
Customer value	Customer value refers to the unique combination of benefits received by targeted buyers that includes quality, price, convenience, on-time delivery, and both before-sale and after-sale service.
Enterprise	Enterprise refers to another name for a business organization. Other similar terms are business firm, sometimes simply business, sometimes simply firm, as well as company, and entity.
Service	Service refers to a "non tangible product" that is not embodied in a physical good and that typically effects some change in another product, person, or institution. Contrasts with good.
Contribution	In business organization law, the cash or property contributed to a business by its owners is referred to as contribution.
Consideration	Consideration in contract law, a basic requirement for an enforceable agreement under traditional contract principles, defined in this text as legal value, bargained for and given in exchange for an act or promise. In corporation law, cash or property contributed to a corporation in exchange for shares, or a promise to contribute such cash or property.
Benchmarking	The continuous process of comparing the levels of performance in producing products and services and executing activities against the best levels of performance is benchmarking.
Scope	Scope of a project is the sum total of all projects products and their requirements or features.
Cooperative	A business owned and controlled by the people who use it, producers, consumers, or workers with similar needs who pool their resources for mutual gain is called cooperative.
Partnership	In the common law, a partnership is a type of business entity in which partners share with each other the profits or losses of the business undertaking in which they have all invested.
Core	A core is the set of feasible allocations in an economy that cannot be improved upon by subset of the set of the economy's consumers (a coalition). In construction, when the force in an element is within a certain center section, the core, the element will only be under compression.
Planning horizon	The length of time it takes to conceive, develop, and complete a project and to recover the cost of the project on a discounted cash flow basis is referred to as planning horizon.
Extension	Extension refers to an out-of-court settlement in which creditors agree to allow the firm more time to meet its financial obligations. A new repayment schedule will be developed,

Go to **Cram101.com** for the Practice Tests for this Chapter.

subject to the acceptance of creditors.

Brief	Brief refers to a statement of a party's case or legal arguments, usually prepared by an attorney. Also used to make legal arguments before appellate courts.
Relational database	Relational database refers to a database structure that stores information in separate files that can be linked by common elements.
Product differentiation	A strategy in which one firm's product is distinguished from competing products by means of its design, related services, quality, location, or other attributes is called product differentiation.
Productivity	Productivity refers to the total output of goods and services in a given period of time divided by work hours.
Assessment	Collecting information and providing feedback to employees about their behavior, communication style, or skills is an assessment.
Strategic congruence	Strategic congruence refers to the extent to which the performance management system elicits job performance that is consistent with the organization's strategy, goals, and culture.
Systems design	Systems design is the process or art of defining the hardware and software architecture, components, modules, interfaces, and data for a computer system to satisfy specified requirements.
Stakeholder	A stakeholder is an individual or group with a vested interest in or expectation for organizational performance. Usually stakeholders can either have an effect on or are affected by an organization.
Enabling	Enabling refers to giving workers the education and tools they need to assume their new decision-making powers.
Trend	Trend refers to the long-term movement of an economic variable, such as its average rate of increase or decrease over enough years to encompass several business cycles.
Rationalization	Rationalization in economics is an attempt to change a pre-existing ad-hoc workflow into one that is based on a set of published rules.
Restructuring	Restructuring is the corporate management term for the act of partially dismantling and reorganizing a company for the purpose of making it more efficient and therefore more profitable.
Downturn	A decline in a stock market or economic cycle is a downturn.
Takeover	A takeover in business refers to one company (the acquirer) purchasing another (the target). Such events resemble mergers, but without the formation of a new company.
Merger	Merger refers to the combination of two firms into a single firm.
Production	The creation of finished goods and services using the factors of production: land, labor, capital, entrepreneurship, and knowledge.
Channel	Channel, in communications (sometimes called communications channel), refers to the medium used to convey information from a sender (or transmitter) to a receiver.
Organizational environment	Organizational environment refers to everything outside an organization. It includes all elements, people, other organizations, economic factors, objects, and events that lie outside the boundaries of the organization.
Composition	An out-of-court settlement in which creditors agree to accept a fractional settlement on their original claim is referred to as composition.
Confirmed	When the seller's bank agrees to assume liability on the letter of credit issued by the

	buyer's bank the transaction is confirmed. The term means that the credit is not only backed up by the issuing foreign bank, but that payment is also guaranteed by the notifying American bank.
Strategic business unit	Strategic business unit is understood as a business unit within the overall corporate identity which is distinguishable from other business because it serves a defined external market where management can conduct strategic planning in relation to products and markets. When companies become really large, they are best thought of as being composed of a number of businesses
Business unit	The lowest level of the company which contains the set of functions that carry a product through its life span from concept through manufacture, distribution, sales and service is a business unit.
Centralization	A structural policy in which decision-making authority is concentrated at the top of the organizational hierarchy is referred to as centralization.
Supply and demand	The partial equilibrium supply and demand economic model originally developed by Alfred Marshall attempts to describe, explain, and predict changes in the price and quantity of goods sold in competitive markets.
Logistics	Those activities that focus on getting the right amount of the right products to the right place at the right time at the lowest possible cost is referred to as logistics.
Business unit level	Level at which business unit managers set the direction for their products and markets is called business unit level.
Corporation	A legal entity chartered by a state or the Federal government that is distinct and separate from the individuals who own it is a corporation. This separation gives the corporation unique powers which other legal entities lack.
Operational strategy	The "lowest" level of strategy is operational strategy. It is very narrow in focus and deals with day-to-day operational activities such as scheduling criteria. It must operate within a budget but is not at liberty to adjust or create that budget.
Reorganization	Reorganization occurs, among other instances, when one corporation acquires another in a merger or acquisition, a single corporation divides into two or more entities, or a corporation makes a substantial change in its capital structure.
Group system	Group system refers to the organization of an advertising agency by dividing it into groups consisting of specialists from various departments such as creative, media, marketing services, and other areas. These groups work together to service particular accounts.
Synergy	Corporate synergy occurs when corporations interact congruently. A corporate synergy refers to a financial benefit that a corporation expects to realize when it merges with or acquires another corporation.
Conglomerate	A conglomerate is a large company that consists of divisions of often seemingly unrelated businesses.
Holding company	A corporation whose purpose or function is to own or otherwise hold the shares of other corporations either for investment or control is called holding company.
Revenue	Revenue is a U.S. business term for the amount of money that a company receives from its activities, mostly from sales of products and/or services to customers.
Holding	The holding is a court's determination of a matter of law based on the issue presented in the particular case. In other words: under this law, with these facts, this result.
Profit	Profit refers to the return to the resource entrepreneurial ability; total revenue minus total cost.

Go to **Cram101.com** for the Practice Tests for this Chapter.

Interest	In finance and economics, interest is the price paid by a borrower for the use of a lender's money. In other words, interest is the amount of paid to "rent" money for a period of time.
Allocation of resources	Allocation of resources refers to the society's decisions on how to divide up its scarce input resources among the different outputs produced in the economy, and among the different firms or other organizations that produce those outputs.
Policy	Similar to a script in that a policy can be a less than completely rational decision-making method. Involves the use of a pre-existing set of decision steps for any problem that presents itself.
Business plan	A detailed written statement that describes the nature of the business, the target market, the advantages the business will have in relation to competition, and the resources and qualifications of the owner is referred to as a business plan.
Learning curve	Learning curve is a function that measures how labor-hours per unit decline as units of production increase because workers are learning and becoming better at their jobs.
Consolidation	The combination of two or more firms, generally of equal size and market power, to form an entirely new entity is a consolidation.
Organization structure	The system of task, reporting, and authority relationships within which the organization does its work is referred to as the organization structure.
Time horizon	A time horizon is a fixed point of time in the future at which point certain processes will be evaluated or assumed to end. It is necessary in an accounting, finance or risk management regime to assign such a fixed horizon time so that alternatives can be evaluated for performance over the same period of time.
Business analysis	Business analysis is a structured methodology that is focused on completely understanding the customer's needs, identifying how best to meet those needs, and then "reinventing" the stream of processes to meet those needs.
Balance	In banking and accountancy, the outstanding balance is the amount of money owned, (or due), that remains in a deposit account (or a loan account) at a given date, after all past remittances, payments and withdrawal have been accounted for. It can be positive (then, in the balance sheet of a firm, it is an asset) or negative (a liability).
Inputs	The inputs used by a firm or an economy are the labor, raw materials, electricity and other resources it uses to produce its outputs.
Business model	A business model is the instrument by which a business intends to generate revenue and profits. It is a summary of how a company means to serve its employees and customers, and involves both strategy (what an business intends to do) as well as an implementation.
Bureaucracy	Bureaucracy refers to an organization with many layers of managers who set rules and regulations and oversee all decisions.
Business process	Business process refers to the individual activities of an enterprise. Processes can be viewed at a high level, for example, 'marketing,' or at the level of detailed subprocesses, for example, 'customer retention.'.
Business case	The business case addresses, at a high level, the business need that a project seeks to resolve. It includes the reasons for the project, the expected business benefits, the options considered (with reasons for rejecting or carrying forward each option), the expected costs of the project, a gap analysis and the expected risks.
Value chain	The sequence of business functions in which usefulness is added to the products or services of a company is a value chain.
Brainstorming	Brainstorming refers to a technique designed to overcome our natural tendency to evaluate and

Go to **Cram101.com** for the Practice Tests for this Chapter.

criticize ideas and thereby reduce the creative output of those ideas. People are encouraged to produce ideas/options without criticizing, often at a very fast pace to minimize our natural tendency to criticize.

Managing director	Managing director is the term used for the chief executive of many limited companies in the United Kingdom, Commonwealth and some other English speaking countries. The title reflects their role as both a member of the Board of Directors but also as the senior manager.
Gain	In finance, gain is a profit or an increase in value of an investment such as a stock or bond. Gain is calculated by fair market value or the proceeds from the sale of the investment minus the sum of the purchase price and all costs associated with it.
Authority	Authority in agency law, refers to an agent's ability to affect his principal's legal relations with third parties. Also used to refer to an actor's legal power or ability to do something. In addition, sometimes used to refer to a statute, case, or other legal source that justifies a particular result.
Audit procedures	Audit procedures are the tasks the internal auditor undertakes for collecting, analyzing, interpreting, and documenting information during an audit. They are the means to attain audit objectives.
Audit	An examination of the financial reports to ensure that they represent what they claim and conform with generally accepted accounting principles is referred to as audit.
Union	A worker association that bargains with employers over wages and working conditions is called a union.
Corporate level	Corporate level refers to level at which top management directs overall strategy for the entire organization.
Precedent	A previously decided court decision that is recognized as authority for the disposition of future decisions is a precedent.
Negotiation	Negotiation is the process whereby interested parties resolve disputes, agree upon courses of action, bargain for individual or collective advantage, and/or attempt to craft outcomes which serve their mutual interests.
Accounting	A system that collects and processes financial information about an organization and reports that information to decision makers is referred to as accounting.
Management accounting	Management accounting measures and reports financial and nonfinancial information that helps managers make decisions to fulfill the goals of an organization. It focuses on internal reporting.
Cost allocation	Cost allocation refers to the process of assigning costs in a cost pool to the appropriate cost objects.
Public sector	Public sector refers to the part of the economy that contains all government entities; government.
Shareholder	A shareholder is an individual or company (including a corporation) that legally owns one or more shares of stock in a joined stock company.
Collateral	Property that is pledged to the lender to guarantee payment in the event that the borrower is unable to make debt payments is called collateral.
Committee	A long-lasting, sometimes permanent team in the organization structure created to deal with tasks that recur regularly is the committee.
Board of directors	The group of individuals elected by the stockholders of a corporation to oversee its operations is a board of directors.

Ad hoc	Ad hoc is a Latin phrase which means "for this purpose." It generally signifies a solution that has been tailored to a specific purpose and is makeshift and non-general, such as a handcrafted network protocol or a specific-purpose equation, as opposed to general solutions.
Help desk	The group in an organization that provides support for both hardware and software. The term is also used in connection with specialized software that supports help desk operations.
Organizational performance	Organizational performance comprises the actual output or results of an organization as measured against its intended outputs (or goals and objectives).
Performance improvement	Performance improvement is the concept of measuring the output of a particular process or procedure then modifying the process or procedure in order to increase the output, increase efficiency, or increase the effectiveness of the process or procedure.
Realization	Realization is the sale of assets when an entity is being liquidated.
Paradox	As used in economics, paradox means something unexpected, rather than the more extreme normal meaning of something seemingly impossible. Some paradoxes are just theoretical results that go against what one thinks of as normal.
Management information system	A computer-based system that provides information and support for effective managerial decision makin is referred to as a management information system.

Deliverable	A deliverable refers to a product created as a result of project work.
Alignment	Term that refers to optimal coordination among disparate departments and divisions within a firm is referred to as alignment.
Technology	The body of knowledge and techniques that can be used to combine economic resources to produce goods and services is called technology.
Assessment	Collecting information and providing feedback to employees about their behavior, communication style, or skills is an assessment.
Gap	In December of 1995, Gap became the first major North American retailer to accept independent monitoring of the working conditions in a contract factory producing its garments. Gap is the largest specialty retailer in the United States.
Strategy formulation	The process of deciding on a strategic direction by defining a company's mission and goals, its external opportunities and threats, and its internal strengths and weaknesses is referred to as a strategy formulation.
Portfolio	In finance, a portfolio is a collection of investments held by an institution or a private individual. Holding but not always a portfolio is part of an investment and risk-limiting strategy called diversification. By owning several assets, certain types of risk (in particular specific risk) can be reduced.
Business process	Business process refers to the individual activities of an enterprise. Processes can be viewed at a high level, for example, 'marketing,' or at the level of detailed subprocesses, for example, 'customer retention.'.
Management	Management characterizes the process of leading and directing all or part of an organization, often a business, through the deployment and manipulation of resources. Early twentieth-century management writer Mary Parker Follett defined management as "the art of getting things done through people."
Ford	Ford is an American company that manufactures and sells automobiles worldwide. Ford introduced methods for large-scale manufacturing of cars, and large-scale management of an industrial workforce, especially elaborately engineered manufacturing sequences typified by the moving assembly lines.
Customer service	The ability of logistics management to satisfy users in terms of time, dependability, communication, and convenience is called the customer service.
Service	Service refers to a "non tangible product" that is not embodied in a physical good and that typically effects some change in another product, person, or institution. Contrasts with good.
Business strategy	Business strategy, which refers to the aggregated operational strategies of single business firm or that of an SBU in a diversified corporation refers to the way in which a firm competes in its chosen arenas.
Contribution	In business organization law, the cash or property contributed to a business by its owners is referred to as contribution.
Partnership	In the common law, a partnership is a type of business entity in which partners share with each other the profits or losses of the business undertaking in which they have all invested.
Subsidiary	A company that is controlled by another company or corporation is a subsidiary.
Innovation	Innovation refers to the first commercially successful introduction of a new product, the use of a new method of production, or the creation of a new form of business organization.
Operation	A standardized method or technique that is performed repetitively, often on different

	materials resulting in different finished goods is called an operation.
Critical success factor	Critical Success Factor is a business term for an element which is necessary for an organization or project to achieve its mission.
Success factor	The term success factor refers to the characteristics necessary for high performance; knowledge, skills, abilities, behaviors.
Supply	Supply is the aggregate amount of any material good that can be called into being at a certain price point; it comprises one half of the equation of supply and demand. In classical economic theory, a curve representing supply is one of the factors that produce price.
Trend	Trend refers to the long-term movement of an economic variable, such as its average rate of increase or decrease over enough years to encompass several business cycles.
Business model	A business model is the instrument by which a business intends to generate revenue and profits. It is a summary of how a company means to serve its employees and customers, and involves both strategy (what an business intends to do) as well as an implementation.
Value chain	The sequence of business functions in which usefulness is added to the products or services of a company is a value chain.
Investment	Investment refers to spending for the production and accumulation of capital and additions to inventories. In a financial sense, buying an asset with the expectation of making a return.
SWOT	SWOT analysis refers to an acronym describing an organization's appraisal of its internal strengths and weaknesses and its external opportunities and threats.
Context	The effect of the background under which a message often takes on more and richer meaning is a context. Context is especially important in cross-cultural interactions because some cultures are said to be high context or low context.
Performance target	A task established for an employee that provides the comparative basis for performance appraisal is a performance target.
Positioning	The art and science of fitting the product or service to one or more segments of the market in such a way as to set it meaningfully apart from competition is called positioning.
Internal environment	Variables that are under some degree of control by organizational members is the internal enviroment. Internal environment scans are conducted to identify an organization's internal capabilities, performance levels, strengths, and weaknesses.
Organizational environment	Organizational environment refers to everything outside an organization. It includes all elements, people, other organizations, economic factors, objects, and events that lie outside the boundaries of the organization.
Tangible	Having a physical existence is referred to as the tangible. Personal property other than real estate, such as cars, boats, stocks, or other assets.
Stock	In financial terminology, stock is the capital raized by a corporation, through the issuance and sale of shares.
Asset	An item of property, such as land, capital, money, a share in ownership, or a claim on others for future payment, such as a bond or a bank deposit is an asset.
Competitor	Other organizations in the same industry or type of business that provide a good or service to the same set of customers is referred to as a competitor.
Market	A market is, as defined in economics, a social arrangement that allows buyers and sellers to discover information and carry out a voluntary exchange of goods or services.
Business unit	The lowest level of the company which contains the set of functions that carry a product

Go to **Cram101.com** for the Practice Tests for this Chapter.

	through its life span from concept through manufacture, distribution, sales and service is a business unit.
Senior management	Senior management is generally a team of individuals at the highest level of organizational management who have the day-to-day responsibilities of managing a corporation.
Confirmed	When the seller's bank agrees to assume liability on the letter of credit issued by the buyer's bank the transaction is confirmed.The term means that the credit is not only backed up by the issuing foreign bank, but that payment is also guaranteed by the notifying American bank.
Brand loyalty	The degree to which customers are satisfied, like the brand, and are committed to further purchase is referred to as brand loyalty.
Loyalty	Marketers tend to define customer loyalty as making repeat purchases. Some argue that it should be defined attitudinally as a strongly positive feeling about the brand.
Brand	A name, symbol, or design that identifies the goods or services of one seller or group of sellers and distinguishes them from the goods and services of competitors is a brand.
Profit	Profit refers to the return to the resource entrepreneurial ability; total revenue minus total cost.
Committee	A long-lasting, sometimes permanent team in the organization structure created to deal with tasks that recur regularly is the committee.
Capital	Capital generally refers to financial wealth, especially that used to start or maintain a business. In classical economics, capital is one of four factors of production, the others being land and labor and entrepreneurship.
Production	The creation of finished goods and services using the factors of production: land, labor, capital, entrepreneurship, and knowledge.
Tactic	A short-term immediate decision that, in its totality, leads to the achievement of strategic goals is called a tactic.
Competitive disadvantage	A situation in which a firm is not implementing using strategies that are being used by competing organizations is competitive disadvantage.
Competitive Strategy	An outline of how a business intends to compete with other firms in the same industry is called competitive strategy.
Organizational structure	Organizational structure is the way in which the interrelated groups of an organization are constructed. From a managerial point of view the main concerns are ensuring effective communication and coordination.
Scope	Scope of a project is the sum total of all projects products and their requirements or features.
Marketing	Promoting and selling products or services to customers, or prospective customers, is referred to as marketing.
Functional organization	Functional organization is a method of organization in which chapters and sections of a manual correspond to business functions, not specific departments or work groups.
Internal customer	An individuals or unit within the firm that receives services from other entities within the organization is an internal customer.
Information system	An information system is a system whether automated or manual, that comprises people, machines, and/or methods organized to collect, process, transmit, and disseminate data that represent user information.

Analyst	Analyst refers to a person or tool with a primary function of information analysis, generally with a more limited, practical and short term set of goals than a researcher.
Enterprise	Enterprise refers to another name for a business organization. Other similar terms are business firm, sometimes simply business, sometimes simply firm, as well as company, and entity.
Industry	A group of firms that produce identical or similar products is an industry. It is also used specifically to refer to an area of economic production focused on manufacturing which involves large amounts of capital investment before any profit can be realized, also called "heavy industry".
Vendor	A person who sells property to a vendee is a vendor. The words vendor and vendee are more commonly applied to the seller and purchaser of real estate, and the words seller and buyer are more commonly applied to the seller and purchaser of personal property.
Strategic business unit	Strategic business unit is understood as a business unit within the overall corporate identity which is distinguishable from other business because it serves a defined external market where management can conduct strategic planning in relation to products and markets. When companies become really large, they are best thought of as being composed of a number of businesses
Rationalization	Rationalization in economics is an attempt to change a pre-existing ad-hoc workflow into one that is based on a set of published rules.
Policy	Similar to a script in that a policy can be a less than completely rational decision-making method. Involves the use of a pre-existing set of decision steps for any problem that presents itself.
Remainder	A remainder in property law is a future interest created in a transferee that is capable of becoming possessory upon the natural termination of a prior estate created by the same instrument.
Evaluation	The consumer's appraisal of the product or brand on important attributes is called evaluation.
Users	Users refer to people in the organization who actually use the product or service purchased by the buying center.
Gain	In finance, gain is a profit or an increase in value of an investment such as a stock or bond. Gain is calculated by fair market value or the proceeds from the sale of the investment minus the sum of the purchase price and all costs associated with it.
Project management	Project management is the discipline of organizing and managing resources in such a way that these resources deliver all the work required to complete a project within defined scope, time, and cost constraints.
Quality assurance	Those activities associated with assuring the quality of a product or service is called quality assurance.
Systems design	Systems design is the process or art of defining the hardware and software architecture, components, modules, interfaces, and data for a computer system to satisfy specified requirements.
Rapid application development	Rapid application development is a software programming technique that allows quick development of software applications. Some rapid application development implementations include visual tools for development and others generate software frameworks through tools known as "wizards".
Expert system	Computer systems incorporating the decision rules of people recognized as experts in a

Go to **Cram101.com** for the Practice Tests for this Chapter.

certain area are refered to as an expert system.

Categorizing	The act of placing strengths and weaknesses into categories in generic internal assessment is called categorizing.
Consideration	Consideration in contract law, a basic requirement for an enforceable agreement under traditional contract principles, defined in this text as legal value, bargained for and given in exchange for an act or promise. In corporation law, cash or property contributed to a corporation in exchange for shares, or a promise to contribute such cash or property.
Business case	The business case addresses, at a high level, the business need that a project seeks to resolve. It includes the reasons for the project, the expected business benefits, the options considered (with reasons for rejecting or carrying forward each option), the expected costs of the project, a gap analysis and the expected risks.
Integration	Economic integration refers to reducing barriers among countries to transactions and to movements of goods, capital, and labor, including harmonization of laws, regulations, and standards. Integrated markets theoretically function as a unified market.
Hierarchy	A system of grouping people in an organization according to rank from the top down in which all subordinate managers must report to one person is called a hierarchy.
Balanced scorecard	A framework for implementing strategy by translating an organization's mission and strategy into a set of performance measures is called balanced scorecard.
Performance measurement	The process by which someone evaluates an employee's work behaviors by measurement and comparison with previously established standards, documents the results, and communicates the results to the employee is called performance measurement.
Financial measure	A financial measure is often used as a very simple mechanism to describe the performance of a business or investment. Because they are easily calculated they can not only be used to compare year on year results but also to compare and set norms for a particular type of business or investment.
Factor analysis	Factor analysis is a statistical technique used to explain variability among observed random variables in terms of fewer unobserved random variables called factors.
Raw material	Raw material refers to a good that has not been transformed by production; a primary product.
Firm	An organization that employs resources to produce a good or service for profit and owns and operates one or more plants is referred to as a firm.
Return on investment	Return on investment refers to the return a businessperson gets on the money he and other owners invest in the firm; for example, a business that earned $100 on a $1,000 investment would have a ROI of 10 percent: 100 divided by 1000.
Diversification	Investing in a collection of assets whose returns do not always move together, with the result that overall risk is lower than for individual assets is referred to as diversification.
Management control	That aspect of management concerned with the comparison of actual versus planned performance as well as the development and implementation of procedures to correct substandard performance is called management control.
Complaint	The pleading in a civil case in which the plaintiff states his claim and requests relief is called complaint. In the common law, it is a formal legal document that sets out the basic facts and legal reasons that the filing party (the plaintiffs) believes are sufficient to support a claim against another person, persons, entity or entities (the defendants) that entitles the plaintiff(s) to a remedy (either money damages or injunctive relief).
Quality	Quality management is a method for ensuring that all the activities necessary to design,

management	develop and implement a product or service are effective and efficient with respect to the system and its performance.
Consolidation	The combination of two or more firms, generally of equal size and market power, to form an entirely new entity is a consolidation.
Comprehensive	A comprehensive refers to a layout accurate in size, color, scheme, and other necessary details to show how a final ad will look. For presentation only, never for reproduction.
Core business	The core business of an organization is an idealized construct intended to express that organization's "main" or "essential" activity.
Core	A core is the set of feasible allocations in an economy that cannot be improved upon by subset of the set of the economy's consumers (a coalition). In construction, when the force in an element is within a certain center section, the core, the element will only be under compression.
Gross profit	Net sales less cost of goods sold is called gross profit.
Channel	Channel, in communications (sometimes called communications channel), refers to the medium used to convey information from a sender (or transmitter) to a receiver.
Margin	A deposit by a buyer in stocks with a seller or a stockbroker, as security to cover fluctuations in the market in reference to stocks that the buyer has purchased but for which he has not paid is a margin. Commodities are also traded on margin.
Option	A contract that gives the purchaser the option to buy or sell the underlying financial instrument at a specified price, called the exercise price or strike price, within a specific period of time.
Agent	A person who makes economic decisions for another economic actor. A hired manager operates as an agent for a firm's owner.
Financial perspective	Financial perspective is one of the four standard perspectives used with the Balanced Scorecard. Financial perspective measures inform an organization whether strategy execution, which is detailed through measures in the other three perspectives, is leading to improved bottom line results.
Organization design	The structuring of workers so that they can best accomplish the firm's goals is referred to as organization design.
Workflow	Workflow refers to automated systems that electronically route documents to the next person in the process.
Purchase order	A form on which items or services needed by a business firm are specified and then communicated to the vendor is a purchase order.
Information technology	Information technology refers to technology that helps companies change business by allowing them to use new methods.
Enabling	Enabling refers to giving workers the education and tools they need to assume their new decision-making powers.
Appeal	Appeal refers to the act of asking an appellate court to overturn a decision after the trial court's final judgment has been entered.
Performance improvement	Performance improvement is the concept of measuring the output of a particular process or procedure then modifying the process or procedure in order to increase the output, increase efficiency, or increase the effectiveness of the process or procedure.
Fund	Independent accounting entity with a self-balancing set of accounts segregated for the purposes of carrying on specific activities is referred to as a fund.

Go to **Cram101.com** for the Practice Tests for this Chapter.

Aid	Assistance provided by countries and by international institutions such as the World Bank to developing countries in the form of monetary grants, loans at low interest rates, in kind, or a combination of these is called aid. Aid can also refer to assistance of any type rendered to benefit some group or individual.
Reengineering	The fundamental rethinking and redesign of business processes to achieve improvements in critical measures of performance, such as cost, quality, service, speed, and customer satisfaction is referred to as reengineering.
Stakeholder	A stakeholder is an individual or group with a vested interest in or expectation for organizational performance. Usually stakeholders can either have an effect on or are affected by an organization.
Competitiveness	Competitiveness usually refers to characteristics that permit a firm to compete effectively with other firms due to low cost or superior technology, perhaps internationally.
Benchmarking	The continuous process of comparing the levels of performance in producing products and services and executing activities against the best levels of performance is benchmarking.
American Express	From the early 1980s until the late 1990s, American Express was known for cutting its merchant fees (also known as a "discount rate") to fine merchants and restaurants if they only accepted American Express and no other credit or charge cards. This prompted competitors such as Visa and MasterCard to cry foul for a while, as the tactics "locked" restaurants into American Express.
Customer relationship management	Learning as much as possible about customers and doing everything you can to satisfy them or even delight them with goods and services over time is customer relationship management.
Relationship management	A method for developing long-term associations with customers is referred to as relationship management.
Customer satisfaction	Customer satisfaction is a business term which is used to capture the idea of measuring how satisfied an enterprise's customers are with the organization's efforts in a marketplace.
Shareholder	A shareholder is an individual or company (including a corporation) that legally owns one or more shares of stock in a joined stock company.
Corporation	A legal entity chartered by a state or the Federal government that is distinct and separate from the individuals who own it is a corporation. This separation gives the corporation unique powers which other legal entities lack.
Tangible asset	Assets that have physical substance that cannot easily be converted into cash are referd to as a tangible asset.
Coalition	An informal alliance among managers who support a specific goal is called coalition.
Variable	A variable is something measured by a number; it is used to analyze what happens to other things when the size of that number changes.
Task environment	Task environment includes specific organizations, groups, and individuals that influence the organization.
Intervention	Intervention refers to an activity in which a government buys or sells its currency in the foreign exchange market in order to affect its currency's exchange rate.
Competitive advantage	A business is said to have a competitive advantage when its unique strengths, often based on cost, quality, time, and innovation, offer consumers a greater percieved value and there by diffetiating it from its competitors.
Intellectual	In law, intellectual property is an umbrella term for various legal entitlements which

property	attach to certain types of information, ideas, or other intangibles in their expressed form. The holder of this legal entitlement is generally entitled to exercise various exclusive rights in relation to its subject matter.
Financial assets	Financial assets refer to monetary claims or obligations by one party against another party. Examples are bonds, mortgages, bank loans, and equities.
Turnover	Turnover in a financial context refers to the rate at which a provider of goods cycles through its average inventory. Turnover in a human resources context refers to the characteristic of a given company or industry, relative to rate at which an employer gains and loses staff.
Property	Assets defined in the broadest legal sense. Property includes the unrealized receivables of a cash basis taxpayer, but not services rendered.
Trade union	A Trade Union, as we understand the term, is a continuous association of wage-earners for the purpose of maintaining or improving the conditions of their employment. They may organise strikes or resistance to lockouts in furtherance of particular goals.
Union	A worker association that bargains with employers over wages and working conditions is called a union.
Customs	Customs is an authority or agency in a country responsible for collecting customs duties and for controlling the flow of people, animals and goods (including personal effects and hazardous items) in and out of the country.
Maturity	Maturity refers to the final payment date of a loan or other financial instrument, after which point no further interest or principal need be paid.
Management information system	A computer-based system that provides information and support for effective managerial decision makin is referred to as a management information system.
Process reengineering	Process reengineering refers to the total rethinking and redesign of organizational process to improve performance and innovation; involves analyzing, streamlining, and reconfiguring actions and tasks to achieve work goals.
Harvard Business Review	Harvard Business Review is a research-based magazine written for business practitioners, it claims a high ranking business readership and enjoys the reverence of academics, executives, and management consultants. It has been the frequent publishing home for well known scholars and management thinkers.
Industrial engineering	Industrial engineering is the engineering discipline that concerns the development, improvement, implementation and evaluation of integrated systems of people, knowledge, equipment, energy, material and process.
Management science	Management science is the discipline of using mathematics, and other analytical methods, to help make better business decisions.
Journal	Book of original entry, in which transactions are recorded in a general ledger system, is referred to as a journal.
HarperCollins	HarperCollins is a publishing organization owned by News Corporation. The company found success in 1841 as a printer of Bibles, and in 1848 Collins's son Sir William Collins developed the firm as a publishing venture, specializing in religious and educational books.
Best practice	Best practice is a management idea which asserts that there is a technique, method, process, activity, incentive or reward that is more effective at delivering a particular outcome than any other technique, method, process, etc.
Manufacturing	Production of goods primarily by the application of labor and capital to raw materials and

Go to **Cram101.com** for the Practice Tests for this Chapter.

	other intermediate inputs, in contrast to agriculture, mining, forestry, fishing, and services a manufacturing.
Configuration	An organization's shape, which reflects the division of labor and the means of coordinating the divided tasks is configuration.
Operations management	A specialized area in management that converts or transforms resources into goods and services is operations management.
Extension	Extension refers to an out-of-court settlement in which creditors agree to allow the firm more time to meet its financial obligations. A new repayment schedule will be developed, subject to the acceptance of creditors.

86

Go to **Cram101.com** for the Practice Tests for this Chapter.

Management control	That aspect of management concerned with the comparison of actual versus planned performance as well as the development and implementation of procedures to correct substandard performance is called management control.
Management	Management characterizes the process of leading and directing all or part of an organization, often a business, through the deployment and manipulation of resources. Early twentieth-century management writer Mary Parker Follett defined management as "the art of getting things done through people."
Assessment	Collecting information and providing feedback to employees about their behavior, communication style, or skills is an assessment.
Competitive disadvantage	A situation in which a firm is not implementing using strategies that are being used by competing organizations is competitive disadvantage.
Success factor	The term success factor refers to the characteristics necessary for high performance; knowledge, skills, abilities, behaviors.
Competitor	Other organizations in the same industry or type of business that provide a good or service to the same set of customers is referred to as a competitor.
Investment	Investment refers to spending for the production and accumulation of capital and additions to inventories. In a financial sense, buying an asset with the expectation of making a return.
Industry	A group of firms that produce identical or similar products is an industry. It is also used specifically to refer to an area of economic production focused on manufacturing which involves large amounts of capital investment before any profit can be realized, also called "heavy industry".
Option	A contract that gives the purchaser the option to buy or sell the underlying financial instrument at a specified price, called the exercise price or strike price, within a specific period of time.
Information system	An information system is a system whether automated or manual, that comprises people, machines, and/or methods organized to collect, process, transmit, and disseminate data that represent user information.
Context	The effect of the background under which a message often takes on more and richer meaning is a context. Context is especially important in cross-cultural interactions because some cultures are said to be high context or low context.
Supply chain	Supply chain refers to the flow of goods, services, and information from the initial sources of materials and services to the delivery of products to consumers.
Supply	Supply is the aggregate amount of any material good that can be called into being at a certain price point; it comprises one half of the equation of supply and demand. In classical economic theory, a curve representing supply is one of the factors that produce price.
Market	A market is, as defined in economics, a social arrangement that allows buyers and sellers to discover information and carry out a voluntary exchange of goods or services.
Business unit	The lowest level of the company which contains the set of functions that carry a product through its life span from concept through manufacture, distribution, sales and service is a business unit.
Portfolio	In finance, a portfolio is a collection of investments held by an institution or a private individual. Holding but not always a portfolio is part of an investment and risk-limiting strategy called diversification. By owning several assets, certain types of risk (in particular specific risk) can be reduced.
Niche	In industry, a niche is a situation or an activity perfectly suited to a person. A niche can

Go to **Cram101.com** for the Practice Tests for this Chapter.

	imply a working position or an area suited to a person who occupies it. Basically, a job where a person is able to succeed and thrive.
Niche market	A niche market or market niche is a focused, targetable portion of a market. By definition, then, a business that focuses on a niche market is addressing a need for a product or service that is not being addressed by mainstream providers.
Allocation of resources	Allocation of resources refers to the society's decisions on how to divide up its scarce input resources among the different outputs produced in the economy, and among the different firms or other organizations that produce those outputs.
Situation analysis	Taking stock of where the fine or product has been recently, where it is now, and where it is headed in terms of the organization's plans and the external factors and trends affecting it is a situation analysis.
Evaluation	The consumer's appraisal of the product or brand on important attributes is called evaluation.
Operational excellence	Operational excellence is a goal of conducting business in a manner that improves quality, obtains higher yields, faster throughput, and less waste.
Leadership	Management merely consists of leadership applied to business situations; or in other words: management forms a sub-set of the broader process of leadership.
Profit	Profit refers to the return to the resource entrepreneurial ability; total revenue minus total cost.
Mortgage	Mortgage refers to a note payable issued for property, such as a house, usually repaid in equal installments consisting of part principle and part interest, over a specified period.
Performance improvement	Performance improvement is the concept of measuring the output of a particular process or procedure then modifying the process or procedure in order to increase the output, increase efficiency, or increase the effectiveness of the process or procedure.
Electronic commerce	Electronic commerce or e-commerce, refers to any activity that uses some form of electronic communication in the inventory, exchange, advertisement, distribution, and payment of goods and services.
Mass customization	A manufacturing environment in which many standardized components are combined to produce custommade products to customer order is referred to as mass customization.
Commerce	Commerce is the exchange of something of value between two entities. It is the central mechanism from which capitalism is derived.
Gain	In finance, gain is a profit or an increase in value of an investment such as a stock or bond. Gain is calculated by fair market value or the proceeds from the sale of the investment minus the sum of the purchase price and all costs associated with it.
Michael Porter	Michael Porter is a leading contributor to strategic management theory, Porter's main academic objectives focus on how a firm or a region, can build a competitive advantage and develop competitive strategy. Porter's strategic system consists primarily of 5 forces analysis, strategic groups, the value chain, and market positioning stratagies.
Value chain	The sequence of business functions in which usefulness is added to the products or services of a company is a value chain.
Service	Service refers to a "non tangible product" that is not embodied in a physical good and that typically effects some change in another product, person, or institution. Contrasts with good.
Firm	An organization that employs resources to produce a good or service for profit and owns and

operates one or more plants is referred to as a firm.

Value system	A value system refers to how an individual or a group of individuals organize their ethical or ideological values. A well-defined value system is a moral code.
Consumption	In Keynesian economics consumption refers to personal consumption expenditure, i.e., the purchase of currently produced goods and services out of income, out of savings (net worth), or from borrowed funds. It refers to that part of disposable income that does not go to saving.
Revenue	Revenue is a U.S. business term for the amount of money that a company receives from its activities, mostly from sales of products and/or services to customers.
Net profit	Net profit is an accounting term which is commonly used in business. It is equal to the gross revenue for a given time period minus associated expenses.
Supply and demand	The partial equilibrium supply and demand economic model originally developed by Alfred Marshall attempts to describe, explain, and predict changes in the price and quantity of goods sold in competitive markets.
Matching	Matching refers to an accounting concept that establishes when expenses are recognized. Expenses are matched with the revenues they helped to generate and are recognized when those revenues are recognized.
Manufactured good	A manufactured good refers to goods that have been processed in any way.
Channel	Channel, in communications (sometimes called communications channel), refers to the medium used to convey information from a sender (or transmitter) to a receiver.
Consideration	Consideration in contract law, a basic requirement for an enforceable agreement under traditional contract principles, defined in this text as legal value, bargained for and given in exchange for an act or promise. In corporation law, cash or property contributed to a corporation in exchange for shares, or a promise to contribute such cash or property.
Intermediaries	Intermediaries specialize in information either to bring together two parties to a transaction or to buy in order to sell again.
Exchange	The trade of things of value between buyer and seller so that each is better off after the trade is called the exchange.
Broker	In commerce, a broker is a party that mediates between a buyer and a seller. A broker who also acts as a seller or as a buyer becomes a principal party to the deal.
Inputs	The inputs used by a firm or an economy are the labor, raw materials, electricity and other resources it uses to produce its outputs.
Administration	Administration refers to the management and direction of the affairs of governments and institutions; a collective term for all policymaking officials of a government; the execution and implementation of public policy.
Stock	In financial terminology, stock is the capital raized by a corporation, through the issuance and sale of shares.
Enabling	Enabling refers to giving workers the education and tools they need to assume their new decision-making powers.
Holding	The holding is a court's determination of a matter of law based on the issue presented in the particular case. In other words: under this law, with these facts, this result.
Invoice	The itemized bill for a transaction, stating the nature of the transaction and its cost. In international trade, the invoice price is often the preferred basis for levying an ad valorem

tariff.

Transaction processing	Computations and calculations used to review and document HRM decisions and practices is transaction processing.
Economics	The social science dealing with the use of scarce resources to obtain the maximum satisfaction of society's virtually unlimited economic wants is an economics.
Customer relationship management	Learning as much as possible about customers and doing everything you can to satisfy them or even delight them with goods and services over time is customer relationship management.
Enterprise resource planning	Computer-based production and operations system that links multiple firms into one integrated production unit is enterprise resource planning.
Relationship management	A method for developing long-term associations with customers is referred to as relationship management.
Enterprise	Enterprise refers to another name for a business organization. Other similar terms are business firm, sometimes simply business, sometimes simply firm, as well as company, and entity.
Gap	In December of 1995, Gap became the first major North American retailer to accept independent monitoring of the working conditions in a contract factory producing its garments. Gap is the largest specialty retailer in the United States.
Total cost	The sum of fixed cost and variable cost is referred to as total cost.
Argument	The discussion by counsel for the respective parties of their contentions on the law and the facts of the case being tried in order to aid the jury in arriving at a correct and just conclusion is called argument.
Disintermedi-tion	A reduction in the flow of funds into the banking system that causes the amount financial intermediation to decline is referred to as disintermediation.
A share	In finance the term A share has two distinct meanings, both relating to securities. The first is a designation for a 'class' of common or preferred stock. A share of common or preferred stock typically has enhanced voting rights or other benefits compared to the other forms of shares that may have been created. The equity structure, or how many types of shares are offered, is determined by the corporate charter.
Dealer	People who link buyers with sellers by buying and selling securities at stated prices are referred to as a dealer.
Layout	Layout refers to the physical arrangement of the various parts of an advertisement including the headline, subheads, illustrations, body copy, and any identifying marks.
Preference	The act of a debtor in paying or securing one or more of his creditors in a manner more favorable to them than to other creditors or to the exclusion of such other creditors is a preference. In the absence of statute, a preference is perfectly good, but to be legal it must be bona fide, and not a mere subterfuge of the debtor to secure a future benefit to himself or to prevent the application of his property to his debts.
Production	The creation of finished goods and services using the factors of production: land, labor, capital, entrepreneurship, and knowledge.
Subcontractor	A subcontractor is an individual or in many cases a business that signs a contract to perform part or all of the obligations of another's contract. A subcontractor is hired by a general or prime contractor to perform a specific task as part of the overall project.

Benetton	Benetton has been known in the United States for producing a long-running series of controversial, sometimes offensive, advertisements that have caused a number of media critics to accuse the company of deliberately creating controversy in order to sell its products. This publicity campaign originated when photographer Oliviero Toscani was given carte blanche by the Benetton management.
Working capital	The dollar difference between total current assets and total current liabilities is called working capital.
Accounts receivable	Accounts receivable is one of a series of accounting transactions dealing with the billing of customers which owe money to a person, company or organization for goods and services that have been provided to the customer. This is typically done in a one person organization by writing an invoice and mailing or delivering it to each customer.
Product design	Product Design is defined as the idea generation, concept development, testing and manufacturing or implementation of a physical object or service. It is possibly the evolution of former discipline name - Industrial Design.
Cash flow	In finance, cash flow refers to the amounts of cash being received and spent by a business during a defined period of time, sometimes tied to a specific project. Most of the time they are being used to determine gaps in the liquid position of a company.
Capital	Capital generally refers to financial wealth, especially that used to start or maintain a business. In classical economics, capital is one of four factors of production, the others being land and labor and entrepreneurship.
Agent	A person who makes economic decisions for another economic actor. A hired manager operates as an agent for a firm's owner.
Cost structure	The relative proportion of an organization's fixed, variable, and mixed costs is referred to as cost structure.
Margin	A deposit by a buyer in stocks with a seller or a stockbroker, as security to cover fluctuations in the market in reference to stocks that the buyer has purchased but for which he has not paid is a margin. Commodities are also traded on margin.
Real value	Real value is the value of anything expressed in money of the day with the effects of inflation removed.
Relationship marketing	Marketing whose goal is to keep individual customers over time by offering them products that exactly meet their requirements is called relationship marketing.
Customer value	Customer value refers to the unique combination of benefits received by targeted buyers that includes quality, price, convenience, on-time delivery, and both before-sale and after-sale service.
Value analysis	Value analysis refers to a systematic appraisal of the design, quality, and performance of a product to reduce purchasing costs.
Marketing	Promoting and selling products or services to customers, or prospective customers, is referred to as marketing.
Technology	The body of knowledge and techniques that can be used to combine economic resources to produce goods and services is called technology.
Acquisition	A company's purchase of the property and obligations of another company is an acquisition.
Market research	Market research is the process of systematic gathering, recording and analyzing of data about customers, competitors and the market. Market research can help create a business plan, launch a new product or service, fine tune existing products and services, expand into new markets etc. It can be used to determine which portion of the population will purchase the

	product/service, based on variables like age, gender, location and income level. It can be found out what market characteristics your target market has.
Trial	An examination before a competent tribunal, according to the law of the land, of the facts or law put in issue in a cause, for the purpose of determining such issue is a trial. When the court hears and determines any issue of fact or law for the purpose of determining the rights of the parties, it may be considered a trial.
Export	In economics, an export is any good or commodity, shipped or otherwise transported out of a country, province, town to another part of the world in a legitimate fashion, typically for use in trade or sale.
Authority	Authority in agency law, refers to an agent's ability to affect his principal's legal relations with third parties. Also used to refer to an actor's legal power or ability to do something. In addition, sometimes used to refer to a statute, case, or other legal source that justifies a particular result.
Buyer	A buyer refers to a role in the buying center with formal authority and responsibility to select the supplier and negotiate the terms of the contract.
Balance	In banking and accountancy, the outstanding balance is the amount of money owned, (or due), that remains in a deposit account (or a loan account) at a given date, after all past remittances, payments and withdrawal have been accounted for. It can be positive (then, in the balance sheet of a firm, it is an asset) or negative (a liability).
Customer loyalty	Marketers tend to define customer loyalty as making repeat purchases. Some argue that it should be defined attitudinally as a strongly positive feeling about the brand.
Comprehensive	A comprehensive refers to a layout accurate in size, color, scheme, and other necessary details to show how a final ad will look. For presentation only, never for reproduction.
Proactive	To be proactive is to act before a situation becomes a source of confrontation or crisis. It is the opposite of "retroactive," which refers to actions taken after an event.
Leverage	Leverage is using given resources in such a way that the potential positive or negative outcome is magnified. In finance, this generally refers to borrowing.
Substitute product	Any product viewed by a consumer as an alternative for other products is a substitute product. The substitution is rarely perfect, and varies from time to time depending on price, availability, etc.
Innovation	Innovation refers to the first commercially successful introduction of a new product, the use of a new method of production, or the creation of a new form of business organization.
Distribution	Distribution in economics, the manner in which total output and income is distributed among individuals or factors.
Joint venture	Joint venture refers to an undertaking by two parties for a specific purpose and duration, taking any of several legal forms.
Contribution	In business organization law, the cash or property contributed to a business by its owners is referred to as contribution.
Business model	A business model is the instrument by which a business intends to generate revenue and profits. It is a summary of how a company means to serve its employees and customers, and involves both strategy (what an business intends to do) as well as an implementation.
Human resource management	The process of evaluating human resource needs, finding people to fill those needs, and getting the best work from each employee by providing the right incentives and job environment, all with the goal of meeting the needs of the firm are called human resource management.

Resource management	Resource management is the efficient and effective deployment of an organization's resources when they are needed. Such resources may include financial resources, inventory, human skills, production resources, or information technology.
Logistics	Those activities that focus on getting the right amount of the right products to the right place at the right time at the lowest possible cost is referred to as logistics.
Operation	A standardized method or technique that is performed repetitively, often on different materials resulting in different finished goods is called an operation.
Channel of distribution	A whole set of marketing intermediaries, such as wholesalers and retailers, who join together to transport and store goods in their path from producers to consumers is referred to as channel of distribution.
Current account	Current account refers to a country's international transactions arising from current flows, as opposed to changes in stocks which are part of the capital account. Includes trade in goods and services plus inflows and outflows of transfers. A current account is a deposit account in the UK and countries with a UK banking heritage.
Outbound	Communications originating inside an organization and destined for customers, prospects, or other people outside the organization are called outbound.
Manufacturing	Production of goods primarily by the application of labor and capital to raw materials and other intermediate inputs, in contrast to agriculture, mining, forestry, fishing, and services a manufacturing.
Warranty	An obligation of a company to replace defective goods or correct any deficiencies in performance or quality of a product is called a warranty.
Financial management	The job of managing a firm's resources so it can meet its goals and objectives is called financial management.
Recruitment	Recruitment refers to the set of activities used to obtain a sufficient number of the right people at the right time; its purpose is to select those who best meet the needs of the organization.
Accounting	A system that collects and processes financial information about an organization and reports that information to decision makers is referred to as accounting.
Quality control	The measurement of products and services against set standards is referred to as quality control.
Promotion	Promotion refers to all the techniques sellers use to motivate people to buy products or services. An attempt by marketers to inform people about products and to persuade them to participate in an exchange.
Sales analysis	A tool for controlling marketing programs using sales records to compare actual results with sales goals and to identify strengths and weaknesses is called sales analysis.
Sales forecasting	Sales forecasting refers to the process of predicting sales of services or goods. The initial step in preparing a master budget.
Capacity planning	The determination and adjustment of the organization's ability to produce products and services to match customer demand is called capacity planning.
Configuration	An organization's shape, which reflects the division of labor and the means of coordinating the divided tasks is configuration.
Value chain activities	Value chain activities refer to Porter's chain of activities, including inbound logistics, production, and outbound logistics.
Value added	The value of output minus the value of all intermediate inputs, representing therefore the

contribution of, and payments to, primary factors of production a value added.

Human resources	Human resources refers to the individuals within the firm, and to the portion of the firm's organization that deals with hiring, firing, training, and other personnel issues.
Service business	A business firm that provides services to consumers, such as accounting and legal services, is referred to as a service business.
Mediation	Mediation consists of a process of alternative dispute resolution in which a (generally) neutral third party using appropriate techniques, assists two or more parties to help them negotiate an agreement, with concrete effects, on a matter of common interest.
Integration	Economic integration refers to reducing barriers among countries to transactions and to movements of goods, capital, and labor, including harmonization of laws, regulations, and standards. Integrated markets theoretically function as a unified market.
Contract	A contract is a "promise" or an "agreement" that is enforced or recognized by the law. In the civil law, a contract is considered to be part of the general law of obligations.
Auction	A preexisting business model that operates successfully on the Internet by announcing an item for sale and permitting multiple purchasers to bid on them under specified rules and condition is an auction.
Customer satisfaction	Customer satisfaction is a business term which is used to capture the idea of measuring how satisfied an enterprise's customers are with the organization's efforts in a marketplace.
Assignment	A transfer of property or some right or interest is referred to as assignment.
Core	A core is the set of feasible allocations in an economy that cannot be improved upon by subset of the set of the economy's consumers (a coalition). In construction, when the force in an element is within a certain center section, the core, the element will only be under compression.
Whole product	A whole product is a generic product augmented by everything that is needed for the customer to have a compelling reason to buy.
Raw material	Raw material refers to a good that has not been transformed by production; a primary product.
Tangible	Having a physical existence is referred to as the tangible. Personal property other than real estate, such as cars, boats, stocks, or other assets.
Core business	The core business of an organization is an idealized construct intended to express that organization's "main" or "essential" activity.
Volatility	Volatility refers to the extent to which an economic variable, such as a price or an exchange rate, moves up and down over time.
Insurance	Insurance refers to a system by which individuals can reduce their exposure to risk of large losses by spreading the risks among a large number of persons.
Policy	Similar to a script in that a policy can be a less than completely rational decision-making method. Involves the use of a pre-existing set of decision steps for any problem that presents itself.
Optimum	Optimum refers to the best. Usually refers to a most preferred choice by consumers subject to a budget constraint or a profit maximizing choice by firms or industry subject to a technological constraint.
Critical success factor	Critical Success Factor is a business term for an element which is necessary for an organization or project to achieve its mission.
Business	A business opportunity involves the sale or lease of any product, service, equipment, etc.

opportunity	that will enable the purchaser-licensee to begin a business
Business strategy	Business strategy, which refers to the aggregated operational strategies of single business firm or that of an SBU in a diversified corporation refers to the way in which a firm competes in its chosen arenas.
Ad hoc	Ad hoc is a Latin phrase which means "for this purpose." It generally signifies a solution that has been tailored to a specific purpose and is makeshift and non-general, such as a handcrafted network protocol or a specific-purpose equation, as opposed to general solutions.
Specialist	A specialist is a trader who makes a market in one or several stocks and holds the limit order book for those stocks.
Senior management	Senior management is generally a team of individuals at the highest level of organizational management who have the day-to-day responsibilities of managing a corporation.

Go to **Cram101.com** for the Practice Tests for this Chapter.

Harvard Business Review	Harvard Business Review is a research-based magazine written for business practitioners, it claims a high ranking business readership and enjoys the reverence of academics, executives, and management consultants. It has been the frequent publishing home for well known scholars and management thinkers.
Value chain	The sequence of business functions in which usefulness is added to the products or services of a company is a value chain.
Market	A market is, as defined in economics, a social arrangement that allows buyers and sellers to discover information and carry out a voluntary exchange of goods or services.
Information system	An information system is a system whether automated or manual, that comprises people, machines, and/or methods organized to collect, process, transmit, and disseminate data that represent user information.
Competitive advantage	A business is said to have a competitive advantage when its unique strengths, often based on cost, quality, time, and innovation, offer consumers a greater percieved value and there by differtiating it from its competitors.
Management	Management characterizes the process of leading and directing all or part of an organization, often a business, through the deployment and manipulation of resources. Early twentieth-century management writer Mary Parker Follett defined management as "the art of getting things done through people."
Strategic management	A philosophy of management that links strategic planning with dayto-day decision making. Strategic management seeks a fit between an organization's external and internal environments.
Journal	Book of original entry, in which transactions are recorded in a general ledger system, is referred to as a journal.
Technology	The body of knowledge and techniques that can be used to combine economic resources to produce goods and services is called technology.
Strategic plan	The formal document that presents the ways and means by which a strategic goal will be achieved is a strategic plan. A long-term flexible plan that does not regulate activities but rather outlines the means to achieve certain results, and provides the means to alter the course of action should the desired ends change.
Investment	Investment refers to spending for the production and accumulation of capital and additions to inventories. In a financial sense, buying an asset with the expectation of making a return.
Misuse	A defense that relieves a seller of product liability if the user abnormally misused the product is called misuse. Products must be designed to protect against foreseeable misuse.
Strategic planning	The process of determining the major goals of the organization and the policies and strategies for obtaining and using resources to achieve those goals is called strategic planning.
Portfolio	In finance, a portfolio is a collection of investments held by an institution or a private individual. Holding but not always a portfolio is part of an investment and risk-limiting strategy called diversification. By owning several assets, certain types of risk (in particular specific risk) can be reduced.
Competitor	Other organizations in the same industry or type of business that provide a good or service to the same set of customers is referred to as a competitor.
Industry	A group of firms that produce identical or similar products is an industry. It is also used specifically to refer to an area of economic production focused on manufacturing which involves large amounts of capital investment before any profit can be realized, also called

"heavy industry".

Balance	In banking and accountancy, the outstanding balance is the amount of money owned, (or due), that remains in a deposit account (or a loan account) at a given date, after all past remittances, payments and withdrawal have been accounted for. It can be positive (then, in the balance sheet of a firm, it is an asset) or negative (a liability).
Gain	In finance, gain is a profit or an increase in value of an investment such as a stock or bond. Gain is calculated by fair market value or the proceeds from the sale of the investment minus the sum of the purchase price and all costs associated with it.
Business strategy	Business strategy, which refers to the aggregated operational strategies of single business firm or that of an SBU in a diversified corporation refers to the way in which a firm competes in its chosen arenas.
Enterprise	Enterprise refers to another name for a business organization. Other similar terms are business firm, sometimes simply business, sometimes simply firm, as well as company, and entity.
Supply	Supply is the aggregate amount of any material good that can be called into being at a certain price point; it comprises one half of the equation of supply and demand. In classical economic theory, a curve representing supply is one of the factors that produce price.
Strategy formulation	The process of deciding on a strategic direction by defining a company's mission and goals, its external opportunities and threats, and its internal strengths and weaknesses is referred to as a strategy formulation.
Business unit	The lowest level of the company which contains the set of functions that carry a product through its life span from concept through manufacture, distribution, sales and service is a business unit.
Contribution	In business organization law, the cash or property contributed to a business by its owners is referred to as contribution.
Inputs	The inputs used by a firm or an economy are the labor, raw materials, electricity and other resources it uses to produce its outputs.
Context	The effect of the background under which a message often takes on more and richer meaning is a context. Context is especially important in cross-cultural interactions because some cultures are said to be high context or low context.
Planning horizon	The length of time it takes to conceive, develop, and complete a project and to recover the cost of the project on a discounted cash flow basis is referred to as planning horizon.
Assessment	Collecting information and providing feedback to employees about their behavior, communication style, or skills is an assessment.
Option	A contract that gives the purchaser the option to buy or sell the underlying financial instrument at a specified price, called the exercise price or strike price, within a specific period of time.
Variable	A variable is something measured by a number; it is used to analyze what happens to other things when the size of that number changes.
Corporation	A legal entity chartered by a state or the Federal government that is distinct and separate from the individuals who own it is a corporation. This separation gives the corporation unique powers which other legal entities lack.
Operation	A standardized method or technique that is performed repetitively, often on different materials resulting in different finished goods is called an operation.

Maturity	Maturity refers to the final payment date of a loan or other financial instrument, after which point no further interest or principal need be paid.
Revenue	Revenue is a U.S. business term for the amount of money that a company receives from its activities, mostly from sales of products and/or services to customers.
Profit	Profit refers to the return to the resource entrepreneurial ability; total revenue minus total cost.
SWOT	SWOT analysis refers to an acronym describing an organization's appraisal of its internal strengths and weaknesses and its external opportunities and threats.
Main product	Product from a joint production process that has a high sales value compared with the sales values of all other products of the joint production process is referred to as main product.
Senior executive	Senior executive means a chief executive officer, chief operating officer, chief financial officer and anyone in charge of a principal business unit or function.
Consideration	Consideration in contract law, a basic requirement for an enforceable agreement under traditional contract principles, defined in this text as legal value, bargained for and given in exchange for an act or promise. In corporation law, cash or property contributed to a corporation in exchange for shares, or a promise to contribute such cash or property.
Stakeholder	A stakeholder is an individual or group with a vested interest in or expectation for organizational performance. Usually stakeholders can either have an effect on or are affected by an organization.
Balanced scorecard	A framework for implementing strategy by translating an organization's mission and strategy into a set of performance measures is called balanced scorecard.
Allocate	Allocate refers to the assignment of income for various tax purposes. A multistate corporation's nonbusiness income usually is distributed to the state where the nonbusiness assets are located; it is not apportioned with the rest of the entity's income.
Critical success factor	Critical Success Factor is a business term for an element which is necessary for an organization or project to achieve its mission.
Success factor	The term success factor refers to the characteristics necessary for high performance; knowledge, skills, abilities, behaviors.
Organizational structure	Organizational structure is the way in which the interrelated groups of an organization are constructed. From a managerial point of view the main concerns are ensuring effective communication and coordination.
Economics	The social science dealing with the use of scarce resources to obtain the maximum satisfaction of society's virtually unlimited economic wants is an economics.
Business opportunity	A business opportunity involves the sale or lease of any product, service, equipment, etc. that will enable the purchaser-licensee to begin a business
Senior management	Senior management is generally a team of individuals at the highest level of organizational management who have the day-to-day responsibilities of managing a corporation.
Interest	In finance and economics, interest is the price paid by a borrower for the use of a lender's money. In other words, interest is the amount of paid to "rent" money for a period of time.
Reorganization	Reorganization occurs, among other instances, when one corporation acquires another in a merger or acquisition, a single corporation divides into two or more entities, or a corporation makes a substantial change in its capital structure.
Foundation	A Foundation is a type of philanthropic organization set up by either individuals or institutions as a legal entity (either as a corporation or trust) with the purpose of

Go to **Cram101.com** for the Practice Tests for this Chapter.

distributing grants to support causes in line with the goals of the foundation.

Value chain activities	Value chain activities refer to Porter's chain of activities, including inbound logistics, production, and outbound logistics.
Organization structure	The system of task, reporting, and authority relationships within which the organization does its work is referred to as the organization structure.
Business value	Business value is an informal term that includes all forms of value that determine the health and well-being of the firm in the long-run.
Core business	The core business of an organization is an idealized construct intended to express that organization's "main" or "essential" activity.
Core	A core is the set of feasible allocations in an economy that cannot be improved upon by subset of the set of the economy's consumers (a coalition). In construction, when the force in an element is within a certain center section, the core, the element will only be under compression.
Recovery	Characterized by rizing output, falling unemployment, rizing profits, and increasing economic activity following a decline is a recovery.
Controlling	A management function that involves determining whether or not an organization is progressing toward its goals and objectives, and taking corrective action if it is not is called controlling.
Acquisition	A company's purchase of the property and obligations of another company is an acquisition.
Management effectiveness	In management, the ultimate measure of management's performance is the metric of management effectiveness which includes; execution, leadership, delegation, return on investment, conflict management, motivation, and consideration.
Cost allocation	Cost allocation refers to the process of assigning costs in a cost pool to the appropriate cost objects.
Accounting	A system that collects and processes financial information about an organization and reports that information to decision makers is referred to as accounting.
Interdependence	The extent to which departments depend on each other for resources or materials to accomplish their tasks is referred to as interdependence.
Situation analysis	Taking stock of where the fine or product has been recently, where it is now, and where it is headed in terms of the organization's plans and the external factors and trends affecting it is a situation analysis.
Comprehensive	A comprehensive refers to a layout accurate in size, color, scheme, and other necessary details to show how a final ad will look. For presentation only, never for reproduction.
Consolidation	The combination of two or more firms, generally of equal size and market power, to form an entirely new entity is a consolidation.
Scope	Scope of a project is the sum total of all projects products and their requirements or features.
Distribution channel	A distribution channel is a chain of intermediaries, each passing a product down the chain to the next organization, before it finally reaches the consumer or end-user.
Distribution	Distribution in economics, the manner in which total output and income is distributed among individuals or factors.
Service	Service refers to a "non tangible product" that is not embodied in a physical good and that typically effects some change in another product, person, or institution. Contrasts with

	good.
Channel	Channel, in communications (sometimes called communications channel), refers to the medium used to convey information from a sender (or transmitter) to a receiver.
Parent company	Parent company refers to the entity that has a controlling influence over another company. It may have its own operations, or it may have been set up solely for the purpose of owning the Subject Company.
Synergy	Corporate synergy occurs when corporations interact congruently. A corporate synergy refers to a financial benefit that a corporation expects to realize when it merges with or acquires another corporation.
Economy	The income, expenditures, and resources that affect the cost of running a business and household are called an economy.

Contribution	In business organization law, the cash or property contributed to a business by its owners is referred to as contribution.
Management	Management characterizes the process of leading and directing all or part of an organization, often a business, through the deployment and manipulation of resources. Early twentieth-century management writer Mary Parker Follett defined management as "the art of getting things done through people."
Portfolio	In finance, a portfolio is a collection of investments held by an institution or a private individual. Holding but not always a portfolio is part of an investment and risk-limiting strategy called diversification. By owning several assets, certain types of risk (in particular specific risk) can be reduced.
Variable	A variable is something measured by a number; it is used to analyze what happens to other things when the size of that number changes.
Complexity	The technical sophistication of the product and hence the amount of understanding required to use it is referred to as complexity. It is the opposite of simplicity.
Supply	Supply is the aggregate amount of any material good that can be called into being at a certain price point; it comprises one half of the equation of supply and demand. In classical economic theory, a curve representing supply is one of the factors that produce price.
Strategy formulation	The process of deciding on a strategic direction by defining a company's mission and goals, its external opportunities and threats, and its internal strengths and weaknesses is referred to as a strategy formulation.
Demand management	The use of fiscal policy and monetary policy to increase or decrease aggregate demand is called demand management.
Diffusion	Diffusion is the process by which a new idea or new product is accepted by the market. The rate of diffusion is the speed that the new idea spreads from one consumer to the next.
Information technology	Information technology refers to technology that helps companies change business by allowing them to use new methods.
Business strategy	Business strategy, which refers to the aggregated operational strategies of single business firm or that of an SBU in a diversified corporation refers to the way in which a firm competes in its chosen arenas.
Assessment	Collecting information and providing feedback to employees about their behavior, communication style, or skills is an assessment.
Technology	The body of knowledge and techniques that can be used to combine economic resources to produce goods and services is called technology.
Adoption	In corporation law, a corporation's acceptance of a pre-incorporation contract by action of its board of directors, by which the corporation becomes liable on the contract, is referred to as adoption.
Business opportunity	A business opportunity involves the sale or lease of any product, service, equipment, etc. that will enable the purchaser-licensee to begin a business
Proactive	To be proactive is to act before a situation becomes a source of confrontation or crisis. It is the opposite of "retroactive," which refers to actions taken after an event.
Competitor	Other organizations in the same industry or type of business that provide a good or service to the same set of customers is referred to as a competitor.
Investment	Investment refers to spending for the production and accumulation of capital and additions to inventories. In a financial sense, buying an asset with the expectation of making a return.

Go to **Cram101.com** for the Practice Tests for this Chapter.

Go to **Cram101.com** for the Practice Tests for this Chapter.
And, **NEVER** highlight a book again!

Innovation	Innovation refers to the first commercially successful introduction of a new product, the use of a new method of production, or the creation of a new form of business organization.
Option	A contract that gives the purchaser the option to buy or sell the underlying financial instrument at a specified price, called the exercise price or strike price, within a specific period of time.
Core	A core is the set of feasible allocations in an economy that cannot be improved upon by subset of the set of the economy's consumers (a coalition). In construction, when the force in an element is within a certain center section, the core, the element will only be under compression.
Operational excellence	Operational excellence is a goal of conducting business in a manner that improves quality, obtains higher yields, faster throughput, and less waste.
Comprehensive	A comprehensive refers to a layout accurate in size, color, scheme, and other necessary details to show how a final ad will look. For presentation only, never for reproduction.
Integration	Economic integration refers to reducing barriers among countries to transactions and to movements of goods, capital, and labor, including harmonization of laws, regulations, and standards. Integrated markets theoretically function as a unified market.
Balance	In banking and accountancy, the outstanding balance is the amount of money owned, (or due), that remains in a deposit account (or a loan account) at a given date, after all past remittances, payments and withdrawal have been accounted for. It can be positive (then, in the balance sheet of a firm, it is an asset) or negative (a liability).
Asset	An item of property, such as land, capital, money, a share in ownership, or a claim on others for future payment, such as a bond or a bank deposit is an asset.
Positioning	The art and science of fitting the product or service to one or more segments of the market in such a way as to set it meaningfully apart from competition is called positioning.
Business value	Business value is an informal term that includes all forms of value that determine the health and well-being of the firm in the long-run.
Users	Users refer to people in the organization who actually use the product or service purchased by the buying center.
Production	The creation of finished goods and services using the factors of production: land, labor, capital, entrepreneurship, and knowledge.
Purchasing	Purchasing refers to the function in a firm that searches for quality material resources, finds the best suppliers, and negotiates the best price for goods and services.
Maturity	Maturity refers to the final payment date of a loan or other financial instrument, after which point no further interest or principal need be paid.
Data warehouse	A Data warehouse is a repository of integrated information, available for queries and analysis. Data and information are extracted from heterogeneous sources as they are generated.
Warehouse	Warehouse refers to a location, often decentralized, that a firm uses to store, consolidate, age, or mix stock; house product-recall programs; or ease tax burdens.
Groupware	Software application that enables multiple users to track, share, and organize information and to work on the same database or document simultaneously is the groupware.
Intranet	Intranet refers to a companywide network, closed to public access, that uses Internet-type technology. A set of communications links within one company that travel over the Internet but are closed to public access.

Go to **Cram101.com** for the Practice Tests for this Chapter.

Profitability analysis	A means of measuring the profitability of the firm's products, customer groups, sales territories, channels of distribution, and order sizes is called profitability analysis.
Manufacturing	Production of goods primarily by the application of labor and capital to raw materials and other intermediate inputs, in contrast to agriculture, mining, forestry, fishing, and services a manufacturing.
Personnel	A collective term for all of the employees of an organization. Personnel is also commonly used to refer to the personnel management function or the organizational unit responsible for administering personnel programs.
Sales analysis	A tool for controlling marketing programs using sales records to compare actual results with sales goals and to identify strengths and weaknesses is called sales analysis.
Ledger	Ledger refers to a specialized accounting book in which information from accounting journals is accumulated into specific categories and posted so that managers can find all the information about one account in the same place.
Evaluation	The consumer's appraisal of the product or brand on important attributes is called evaluation.
Firm	An organization that employs resources to produce a good or service for profit and owns and operates one or more plants is referred to as a firm.
Free market	A free market is a market where price is determined by the unregulated interchange of supply and demand rather than set by artificial means.
Monopoly	A monopoly is defined as a persistent market situation where there is only one provider of a kind of product or service.
Market	A market is, as defined in economics, a social arrangement that allows buyers and sellers to discover information and carry out a voluntary exchange of goods or services.
Points	Loan origination fees that may be deductible as interest by a buyer of property. A seller of property who pays points reduces the selling price by the amount of the points paid for the buyer.
Senior management	Senior management is generally a team of individuals at the highest level of organizational management who have the day-to-day responsibilities of managing a corporation.
Organization structure	The system of task, reporting, and authority relationships within which the organization does its work is referred to as the organization structure.
Gain	In finance, gain is a profit or an increase in value of an investment such as a stock or bond. Gain is calculated by fair market value or the proceeds from the sale of the investment minus the sum of the purchase price and all costs associated with it.
Authority	Authority in agency law, refers to an agent's ability to affect his principal's legal relations with third parties. Also used to refer to an actor's legal power or ability to do something. In addition, sometimes used to refer to a statute, case, or other legal source that justifies a particular result.
Conversion	Conversion refers to any distinct act of dominion wrongfully exerted over another's personal property in denial of or inconsistent with his rights therein. That tort committed by a person who deals with chattels not belonging to him in a manner that is inconsistent with the ownership of the lawful owner.
Compliance	A type of influence process where a receiver accepts the position advocated by a source to obtain favorable outcomes or to avoid punishment is the compliance.
Industry	A group of firms that produce identical or similar products is an industry. It is also used

specifically to refer to an area of economic production focused on manufacturing which involves large amounts of capital investment before any profit can be realized, also called "heavy industry".

Context	The effect of the background under which a message often takes on more and richer meaning is a context. Context is especially important in cross-cultural interactions because some cultures are said to be high context or low context.
Euro	The common currency of a subset of the countries of the EU, adopted January 1, 1999 is called euro.
Fund	Independent accounting entity with a self-balancing set of accounts segregated for the purposes of carrying on specific activities is referred to as a fund.
Specialist	A specialist is a trader who makes a market in one or several stocks and holds the limit order book for those stocks.
Functional manager	A manager who is responsible for a department that performs a single functional task and has employees with similar training and skills is referred to as a functional manager.
Budget	Budget refers to an account, usually for a year, of the planned expenditures and the expected receipts of an entity. For a government, the receipts are tax revenues.
Expense	In accounting, an expense represents an event in which an asset is used up or a liability is incurred. In terms of the accounting equation, expenses reduce owners' equity.
Audit	An examination of the financial reports to ensure that they represent what they claim and conform with generally accepted accounting principles is referred to as audit.
Explicit knowledge	Explicit knowledge is knowledge that has been or can be articulated, codified, and stored in certain media. The most common forms of explicit knowledge are manuals, documents, procedures, and stories. Knowledge also can be audio-visual.
Centralization	A structural policy in which decision-making authority is concentrated at the top of the organizational hierarchy is referred to as centralization.
Central planning	The guidance of the economy by direct government control over a large portion of economic activity, as contrasted with allowing markets to serve this purpose is called central planning.
Correlation	A correlation is the measure of the extent to which two economic or statistical variables move together, normalized so that its values range from -1 to +1. It is defined as the covariance of the two variables divided by the square root of the product of their variances.
Administration	Administration refers to the management and direction of the affairs of governments and institutions; a collective term for all policymaking officials of a government; the execution and implementation of public policy.
Automation	Automation allows machines to do work previously accomplished by people.
Boston Consulting Group	The Boston Consulting Group is a management consulting firm founded by Harvard Business School alum Bruce Henderson in 1963. In 1965 Bruce Henderson thought that to survive, much less grow, in a competitive landscape occupied by hundreds of larger and better-known consulting firms, a distinctive identity was needed, and pioneered "Business Strategy" as a special area of expertise.
Service	Service refers to a "non tangible product" that is not embodied in a physical good and that typically effects some change in another product, person, or institution. Contrasts with good.
Cash cow	A cash cow is a product or a business unit that generates unusually high profit margins: so

	high that it is responsible for a large amount of a company's operating profit.
Depreciate	A nation's currency is said to depreciate when exchange rates change so that a unit of its currency can buy fewer units of foreign currency.
Transition management	The process of systematically planning, organizing, and implementing change is called transition management.
Product design	Product Design is defined as the idea generation, concept development, testing and manufacturing or implementation of a physical object or service. It is possibly the evolution of former discipline name - Industrial Design.
Prototyping	An iterative approach to design in which a series of mock-ups or models are developed until the customer and the designer come to agreement as to the final design is called prototyping.
Knowledge management	Sharing, organizing and disseminating information in the simplest and most relevant way possible for the users of the information is a knowledge management.
Electronic commerce	Electronic commerce or e-commerce, refers to any activity that uses some form of electronic communication in the inventory, exchange, advertisement, distribution, and payment of goods and services.
Prototype	A prototype is built to test the function of a new design before starting production of a product.
Commerce	Commerce is the exchange of something of value between two entities. It is the central mechanism from which capitalism is derived.
Vertical integration	Vertical integration refers to production of different stages of processing of a product within the same firm.
Business process	Business process refers to the individual activities of an enterprise. Processes can be viewed at a high level, for example, 'marketing,' or at the level of detailed subprocesses, for example, 'customer retention.'.
Business unit	The lowest level of the company which contains the set of functions that carry a product through its life span from concept through manufacture, distribution, sales and service is a business unit.
Leverage	Leverage is using given resources in such a way that the potential positive or negative outcome is magnified. In finance, this generally refers to borrowing.
Diminishing returns	The fall in the marginal product of a factor or factors that eventually occurs as input of that factor rises, holding the input of at least one other factor fixed, according to the Law of Diminishing Returns.
Matching	Matching refers to an accounting concept that establishes when expenses are recognized. Expenses are matched with the revenues they helped to generate and are recognized when those revenues are recognized.
Compromise	Compromise occurs when the interaction is moderately important to meeting goals and the goals are neither completely compatible nor completely incompatible.
Quality management	Quality management is a method for ensuring that all the activities necessary to design, develop and implement a product or service are effective and efficient with respect to the system and its performance.
Outsourcing	Outsourcing refers to a production activity that was previously done inside a firm or plant that is now conducted outside that firm or plant.
Operation	A standardized method or technique that is performed repetitively, often on different materials resulting in different finished goods is called an operation.

Competitive advantage	A business is said to have a competitive advantage when its unique strengths, often based on cost, quality, time, and innovation, offer consumers a greater percieved value and there by diffetiating it from its competitors.
Profit	Profit refers to the return to the resource entrepreneurial ability; total revenue minus total cost.
Information system	An information system is a system whether automated or manual, that comprises people, machines, and/or methods organized to collect, process, transmit, and disseminate data that represent user information.
Contract	A contract is a "promise" or an "agreement" that is enforced or recognized by the law. In the civil law, a contract is considered to be part of the general law of obligations.
Organizational structure	Organizational structure is the way in which the interrelated groups of an organization are constructed. From a managerial point of view the main concerns are ensuring effective communication and coordination.
Quality control	The measurement of products and services against set standards is referred to as quality control.
Status quo	Status quo is a Latin term meaning the present, current, existing state of affairs.
Resource management	Resource management is the efficient and effective deployment of an organization's resources when they are needed. Such resources may include financial resources, inventory, human skills, production resources, or information technology.
Entrepreneur	The owner/operator. The person who organizes, manages, and assumes the risks of a firm, taking a new idea or a new product and turning it into a successful business is an entrepreneur.
Controller	Controller refers to the financial executive primarily responsible for management accounting and financial accounting. Also called chief accounting officer.
Economy	The income, expenditures, and resources that affect the cost of running a business and household are called an economy.
Retail company	Retail company refers to a merchandizing company that buys goods, adds value, and sells the goods to consumers.
Consumer good	Products and services that are ultimately consumed rather than used in the production of another good are a consumer good.
Distribution	Distribution in economics, the manner in which total output and income is distributed among individuals or factors.
Inventory	Tangible property held for sale in the normal course of business or used in producing goods or services for sale is an inventory.
Customer service	The ability of logistics management to satisfy users in terms of time, dependability, communication, and convenience is called the customer service.
Holding	The holding is a court's determination of a matter of law based on the issue presented in the particular case. In other words: under this law, with these facts, this result.
Stock	In financial terminology, stock is the capital raized by a corporation, through the issuance and sale of shares.
Yield	The interest rate that equates a future value or an annuity to a given present value is a yield.
Financial	A process in which a firm periodically compares its actual revenues, costs, and expenses with

control	its projected ones is called financial control.
Control system	A control system is a device or set of devices that manage the behavior of other devices. Some devices or systems are not controllable.A control system is an interconnection of components connected or related in such a manner as to command, direct, or regulate itself or another system.
Conglomerate	A conglomerate is a large company that consists of divisions of often seemingly unrelated businesses.
Acquisition	A company's purchase of the property and obligations of another company is an acquisition.
Divestment	In finance and economics, divestment or divestiture is the reduction of some kind of asset, for either financial or social goals. A divestment is the opposite of an investment.
Synergy	Corporate synergy occurs when corporations interact congruently. A corporate synergy refers to a financial benefit that a corporation expects to realize when it merges with or acquires another corporation.
Utility	Utility refers to the want-satisfying power of a good or service; the satisfaction or pleasure a consumer obtains from the consumption of a good or service.
Facilitation	Facilitation refers to helping a team or individual achieve a goal. Often used in meetings or with teams to help the teams achieve their objectives.
Strategic management	A philosophy of management that links strategic planning with dayto-day decision making. Strategic management seeks a fit between an organization's external and internal environments.
Harvard Business Review	Harvard Business Review is a research-based magazine written for business practitioners, it claims a high ranking business readership and enjoys the reverence of academics, executives, and management consultants. It has been the frequent publishing home for well known scholars and management thinkers.
Journal	Book of original entry, in which transactions are recorded in a general ledger system, is referred to as a journal.

Inputs	The inputs used by a firm or an economy are the labor, raw materials, electricity and other resources it uses to produce its outputs.
Management	Management characterizes the process of leading and directing all or part of an organization, often a business, through the deployment and manipulation of resources. Early twentieth-century management writer Mary Parker Follett defined management as "the art of getting things done through people."
Portfolio	In finance, a portfolio is a collection of investments held by an institution or a private individual. Holding but not always a portfolio is part of an investment and risk-limiting strategy called diversification. By owning several assets, certain types of risk (in particular specific risk) can be reduced.
Strategic management	A philosophy of management that links strategic planning with dayto-day decision making. Strategic management seeks a fit between an organization's external and internal environments.
Outsourcing	Outsourcing refers to a production activity that was previously done inside a firm or plant that is now conducted outside that firm or plant.
Economics	The social science dealing with the use of scarce resources to obtain the maximum satisfaction of society's virtually unlimited economic wants is an economics.
Service	Service refers to a "non tangible product" that is not embodied in a physical good and that typically effects some change in another product, person, or institution. Contrasts with good.
Supply	Supply is the aggregate amount of any material good that can be called into being at a certain price point; it comprises one half of the equation of supply and demand. In classical economic theory, a curve representing supply is one of the factors that produce price.
Option	A contract that gives the purchaser the option to buy or sell the underlying financial instrument at a specified price, called the exercise price or strike price, within a specific period of time.
Enabling	Enabling refers to giving workers the education and tools they need to assume their new decision-making powers.
Context	The effect of the background under which a message often takes on more and richer meaning is a context. Context is especially important in cross-cultural interactions because some cultures are said to be high context or low context.
Realization	Realization is the sale of assets when an entity is being liquidated.
Policy	Similar to a script in that a policy can be a less than completely rational decision-making method. Involves the use of a pre-existing set of decision steps for any problem that presents itself.
Strategy formulation	The process of deciding on a strategic direction by defining a company's mission and goals, its external opportunities and threats, and its internal strengths and weaknesses is referred to as a strategy formulation.
Decentralization	Decentralization is the process of redistributing decision-making closer to the point of service or action. This gives freedom to managers at lower levels of the organization to make decisions.
Alignment	Term that refers to optimal coordination among disparate departments and divisions within a firm is referred to as alignment.
Disintegration	Disintegration is an organization of production in which different stages of production are divided among different suppliers that are located in different countries.

Go to **Cram101.com** for the Practice Tests for this Chapter.

Investment	Investment refers to spending for the production and accumulation of capital and additions to inventories. In a financial sense, buying an asset with the expectation of making a return.
Centralization	A structural policy in which decision-making authority is concentrated at the top of the organizational hierarchy is referred to as centralization.
Balance	In banking and accountancy, the outstanding balance is the amount of money owned, (or due), that remains in a deposit account (or a loan account) at a given date, after all past remittances, payments and withdrawal have been accounted for. It can be positive (then, in the balance sheet of a firm, it is an asset) or negative (a liability).
Delegation	Delegation is the handing of a task over to another person, usually a subordinate. It is the assignment of authority and responsibility to another person to carry out specific activities.
Information system	An information system is a system whether automated or manual, that comprises people, machines, and/or methods organized to collect, process, transmit, and disseminate data that represent user information.
Rationalization	Rationalization in economics is an attempt to change a pre-existing ad-hoc workflow into one that is based on a set of published rules.
Technology	The body of knowledge and techniques that can be used to combine economic resources to produce goods and services is called technology.
Interest	In finance and economics, interest is the price paid by a borrower for the use of a lender's money. In other words, interest is the amount of paid to "rent" money for a period of time.
Synergy	Corporate synergy occurs when corporations interact congruently. A corporate synergy refers to a financial benefit that a corporation expects to realize when it merges with or acquires another corporation.
Business unit	The lowest level of the company which contains the set of functions that carry a product through its life span from concept through manufacture, distribution, sales and service is a business unit.
PeopleSoft	PeopleSoft, Inc. was a software company that provided HRMS (human resource management), CRM), Manufacturing, Financials, EPM and Student Administration software solutions to large corporations, governments, and organizations. PeopleSoft was acquired in a hostile takeover by the Oracle Corporation.
Vendor	A person who sells property to a vendee is a vendor. The words vendor and vendee are more commonly applied to the seller and purchaser of real estate, and the words seller and buyer are more commonly applied to the seller and purchaser of personal property.
Edict	Edict refers to a command or prohibition promulgated by a sovereign and having the effect of
Baan	In 1998 the Baan Corporation was exposed to be manipulating profits in a prelude to the big accounting scandals that marked the turn of the century. First Paul Baan left the company as a result of this, shortly after to be followed by brother Jan. The loss of confidence in the Baan Corporation was reflected in a rapidly declining share of the BaaN program in the ERP market.
Accounting	A system that collects and processes financial information about an organization and reports that information to decision makers is referred to as accounting.
Committee	A long-lasting, sometimes permanent team in the organization structure created to deal with tasks that recur regularly is the committee.
Private sector	The households and business firms of the economy are referred to as private sector.

Organizational structure	Organizational structure is the way in which the interrelated groups of an organization are constructed. From a managerial point of view the main concerns are ensuring effective communication and coordination.
Positioning	The art and science of fitting the product or service to one or more segments of the market in such a way as to set it meaningfully apart from competition is called positioning.
Corporate Strategy	Corporate strategy is concerned with the firm's choice of business, markets and activities and thus it defines the overall scope and direction of the business.
Enterprise	Enterprise refers to another name for a business organization. Other similar terms are business firm, sometimes simply business, sometimes simply firm, as well as company, and entity.
Exchange	The trade of things of value between buyer and seller so that each is better off after the trade is called the exchange.
Maturity	Maturity refers to the final payment date of a loan or other financial instrument, after which point no further interest or principal need be paid.
Trend	Trend refers to the long-term movement of an economic variable, such as its average rate of increase or decrease over enough years to encompass several business cycles.
Reorganization	Reorganization occurs, among other instances, when one corporation acquires another in a merger or acquisition, a single corporation divides into two or more entities, or a corporation makes a substantial change in its capital structure.
Trust	An arrangement in which shareholders of independent firms agree to give up their stock in exchange for trust certificates that entitle them to a share of the trust's common profits.
Operation	A standardized method or technique that is performed repetitively, often on different materials resulting in different finished goods is called an operation.
Gain	In finance, gain is a profit or an increase in value of an investment such as a stock or bond. Gain is calculated by fair market value or the proceeds from the sale of the investment minus the sum of the purchase price and all costs associated with it.
Conglomerate	A conglomerate is a large company that consists of divisions of often seemingly unrelated businesses.
Leadership	Management merely consists of leadership applied to business situations; or in other words: management forms a sub-set of the broader process of leadership.
Specialist	A specialist is a trader who makes a market in one or several stocks and holds the limit order book for those stocks.
Diffusion	Diffusion is the process by which a new idea or new product is accepted by the market. The rate of diffusion is the speed that the new idea spreads from one consumer to the next.
Cost centre	A cost centre is a division that add to the cost of the organization, but only indirectly add to the profit of the company. Examples include Research and Development, Marketing and Customer service. A cost center is often identified with a speed type number.
Business opportunity	A business opportunity involves the sale or lease of any product, service, equipment, etc. that will enable the purchaser-licensee to begin a business
Revenue	Revenue is a U.S. business term for the amount of money that a company receives from its activities, mostly from sales of products and/or services to customers.
Profit	Profit refers to the return to the resource entrepreneurial ability; total revenue minus total cost.

Go to **Cram101.com** for the Practice Tests for this Chapter.

Users	Users refer to people in the organization who actually use the product or service purchased by the buying center.
Innovation	Innovation refers to the first commercially successful introduction of a new product, the use of a new method of production, or the creation of a new form of business organization.
Business strategy	Business strategy, which refers to the aggregated operational strategies of single business firm or that of an SBU in a diversified corporation refers to the way in which a firm competes in its chosen arenas.
Project management	Project management is the discipline of organizing and managing resources in such a way that these resources deliver all the work required to complete a project within defined scope, time, and cost constraints.
Business process	Business process refers to the individual activities of an enterprise. Processes can be viewed at a high level, for example, 'marketing,' or at the level of detailed subprocesses, for example, 'customer retention.'.
Purchasing	Purchasing refers to the function in a firm that searches for quality material resources, finds the best suppliers, and negotiates the best price for goods and services.
Contract	A contract is a "promise" or an "agreement" that is enforced or recognized by the law. In the civil law, a contract is considered to be part of the general law of obligations.
Authority	Authority in agency law, refers to an agent's ability to affect his principal's legal relations with third parties. Also used to refer to an actor's legal power or ability to do something. In addition, sometimes used to refer to a statute, case, or other legal source that justifies a particular result.
Market	A market is, as defined in economics, a social arrangement that allows buyers and sellers to discover information and carry out a voluntary exchange of goods or services.
Security	Security refers to a claim on the borrower future income that is sold by the borrower to the lender. A security is a type of transferable interest representing financial value.
Conformance	A dimension of quality that refers to the extent to which a product lies within an allowable range of deviation from its specification is called the conformance.
Best practice	Best practice is a management idea which asserts that there is a technique, method, process, activity, incentive or reward that is more effective at delivering a particular outcome than any other technique, method, process, etc.
Consultant	A professional that provides expert advice in a particular field or area in which customers occassionaly require this type of knowledge is a consultant.
Discount	The difference between the face value of a bond and its selling price, when a bond is sold for less than its face value it's referred to as a discount.
Industry	A group of firms that produce identical or similar products is an industry. It is also used specifically to refer to an area of economic production focused on manufacturing which involves large amounts of capital investment before any profit can be realized, also called "heavy industry".
Staffing	Staffing refers to a management function that includes hiring, motivating, and retaining the best people available to accomplish the company's objectives.
Asset	An item of property, such as land, capital, money, a share in ownership, or a claim on others for future payment, such as a bond or a bank deposit is an asset.
Corporate policy	Dimension of social responsibility that refers to the position a firm takes on social and political issues is referred to as corporate policy.

Go to **Cram101.com** for the Practice Tests for this Chapter.

Insourcing	Insourcing refers to process of producing goods or providing services within the organization rather than purchasing those same goods or services from outside vendors.
Human resources	Human resources refers to the individuals within the firm, and to the portion of the firm's organization that deals with hiring, firing, training, and other personnel issues.
Data processing	Data processing refers to a name for business technology in the 1970s; included technology that supported an existing business and was primarily used to improve the flow of financial information.
Personnel	A collective term for all of the employees of an organization. Personnel is also commonly used to refer to the personnel management function or the organizational unit responsible for administering personnel programs.
Eastman Kodak	Eastman Kodak Company is an American multinational public company producing photographic materials and equipment. Long known for its wide range of photographic film products, it has focused in recent years on three main businesses: digital photography, health imaging, and printing. This company remains the largest supplier of films in the world, both for the amateur and professional markets.
Variable	A variable is something measured by a number; it is used to analyze what happens to other things when the size of that number changes.
Public sector	Public sector refers to the part of the economy that contains all government entities; government.
Economy	The income, expenditures, and resources that affect the cost of running a business and household are called an economy.
Confirmed	When the seller's bank agrees to assume liability on the letter of credit issued by the buyer's bank the transaction is confirmed. The term means that the credit is not only backed up by the issuing foreign bank, but that payment is also guaranteed by the notifying American bank.
Budget	Budget refers to an account, usually for a year, of the planned expenditures and the expected receipts of an entity. For a government, the receipts are tax revenues.
Economies of scale	In economics, returns to scale and economies of scale are related terms that describe what happens as the scale of production increases. They are different terms and not to be used interchangeably.
Acquisition	A company's purchase of the property and obligations of another company is an acquisition.
Fixed cost	The cost that a firm bears if it does not produce at all and that is independent of its output. The presence of a fixed cost tends to imply increasing returns to scale. Contrasts with variable cost.
Incremental cost	Additional total cost incurred for an activity is called incremental cost. A form of costing that classifies costs into their fixed and variable elements in order to calculate the extra cost of making and selling an additional batch of units.
Capital asset	In accounting, a capital asset is an asset that is recorded as property that creates more property, e.g. a factory that creates shoes, or a forest that yields a quantity of wood.
Balance sheet	A statement of the assets, liabilities, and net worth of a firm or individual at some given time often at the end of its "fiscal year," is referred to as a balance sheet.
Capital	Capital generally refers to financial wealth, especially that used to start or maintain a business. In classical economics, capital is one of four factors of production, the others being land and labor and entrepreneurship.

Go to **Cram101.com** for the Practice Tests for this Chapter.

Operating budget	An operating budget is the annual budget of an activity stated in terms of Budget Classification Code, functional/subfunctional categories and cost accounts. It contains estimates of the total value of resources required for the performance of the operation including reimbursable work or services for others.
Capital budget	A long-term budget that shows planned acquisition and disposal of capital assets, such as land, building, and equipment is a capital budget. Also a separate budget used by state governments for items such as new construction, major renovations, and acquisition of physical property.
Return on equity	Net profit after taxes per dollar of equity capital is referred to as return on equity.
Equity	Equity is the name given to the set of legal principles, in countries following the English common law tradition, which supplement strict rules of law where their application would operate harshly, so as to achieve what is sometimes referred to as "natural justice."
Information technology	Information technology refers to technology that helps companies change business by allowing them to use new methods.
Mergers and acquisitions	The phrase mergers and acquisitions refers to the aspect of corporate finance strategy and management dealing with the merging and acquiring of different companies as well as other assets. Usually mergers occur in a friendly setting where executives from the respective companies participate in a due diligence process to ensure a successful combination of all parts.
Merger	Merger refers to the combination of two firms into a single firm.
Firm	An organization that employs resources to produce a good or service for profit and owns and operates one or more plants is referred to as a firm.
Harvard Business Review	Harvard Business Review is a research-based magazine written for business practitioners, it claims a high ranking business readership and enjoys the reverence of academics, executives, and management consultants. It has been the frequent publishing home for well known scholars and management thinkers.
Incentive	An incentive is any factor (financial or non-financial) that provides a motive for a particular course of action, or counts as a reason for preferring one choice to the alternatives.
Chief executive officer	A chief executive officer is the highest-ranking corporate officer or executive officer of a corporation, or agency. In closely held corporations, it is general business culture that the office chief executive officer is also the chairman of the board.
Default	In finance, default occurs when a debtor has not met its legal obligations according to the debt contract, e.g. it has not made a scheduled payment, or violated a covenant (condition) of the debt contract.
Chief information officer	The chief information officer is a job title for the head of information technology group within an organization. They often report to the chief executive officer or chief financial officer.
Finance director	Finance director refers to see chief financial officer in charge of financial accounting. Measures and records business transactions and provides financial statements that are based on generally accepted accounting principles.
Argument	The discussion by counsel for the respective parties of their contentions on the law and the facts of the case being tried in order to aid the jury in arriving at a correct and just conclusion is called argument.
Financial	The job of managing a firm's resources so it can meet its goals and objectives is called

management	financial management.
Manufacturing	Production of goods primarily by the application of labor and capital to raw materials and other intermediate inputs, in contrast to agriculture, mining, forestry, fishing, and services a manufacturing.
Business development	Business development emcompasses a number of techniques designed to grow an economic enterprise. Such techniques include, but are not limited to, assessments of marketing opportunities and target markets, intelligence gathering on customers and competitors, generating leads for possible sales, followup sales activity, and formal proposal writing.
Organization chart	Organization chart refers to a visual device, which shows the relationship and divides the organization's work; it shows who is accountable for the completion of specific work and who reports to whom.
Middle management	Middle management refers to the level of management that includes general managers, division managers, and branch and plant managers who are responsible for tactical planning and controlling.
Integration	Economic integration refers to reducing barriers among countries to transactions and to movements of goods, capital, and labor, including harmonization of laws, regulations, and standards. Integrated markets theoretically function as a unified market.
Organization structure	The system of task, reporting, and authority relationships within which the organization does its work is referred to as the organization structure.
Formal organization	Formal organization refers to the structure that details lines of responsibility, authority, and position; that is, the structure shown on organization charts.
Coalition	An informal alliance among managers who support a specific goal is called coalition.
Senior executive	Senior executive means a chief executive officer, chief operating officer, chief financial officer and anyone in charge of a principal business unit or function.
Jargon	Jargon is terminology, much like slang, that relates to a specific activity, profession, or group. It develops as a kind of shorthand, to express ideas that are frequently discussed between members of a group, and can also have the effect of distinguishing those belonging to a group from those who are not.
Senior management	Senior management is generally a team of individuals at the highest level of organizational management who have the day-to-day responsibilities of managing a corporation.
Mature stage	The fourth stage of the product life cycle where sales volume peaks, costs are low, there is an increase in competition and profit is high is the mature stage.
Points	Loan origination fees that may be deductible as interest by a buyer of property. A seller of property who pays points reduces the selling price by the amount of the points paid for the buyer.
Bureaucracy	Bureaucracy refers to an organization with many layers of managers who set rules and regulations and oversee all decisions.
Credibility	The extent to which a source is perceived as having knowledge, skill, or experience relevant to a communication topic and can be trusted to give an unbiased opinion or present objective information on the issue is called credibility.
Supply and demand	The partial equilibrium supply and demand economic model originally developed by Alfred Marshall attempts to describe, explain, and predict changes in the price and quantity of goods sold in competitive markets.
Continuity	A media scheduling strategy where a continuous pattern of advertising is used over the time

span of the advertising campaign is continuity.

Free market	A free market is a market where price is determined by the unregulated interchange of supply and demand rather than set by artificial means.
Relevant cost	A relevant cost refers to expected future costs that differ among alternative courses of action being considered. A cost that will be affected by taking a particular decision.
Financial budget	Financial budget refers to a schedule that outlines how an organization will acquire financial resources during the budget period.
Business plan	A detailed written statement that describes the nature of the business, the target market, the advantages the business will have in relation to competition, and the resources and qualifications of the owner is referred to as a business plan.
Project manager	Project manager refers to a manager responsible for a temporary work project that involves the participation of other people from various functions and levels of the organization.
Management team	A management team is directly responsible for managing the day-to-day operations (and profitability) of a company.
Production	The creation of finished goods and services using the factors of production: land, labor, capital, entrepreneurship, and knowledge.
Loyalty	Marketers tend to define customer loyalty as making repeat purchases. Some argue that it should be defined attitudinally as a strongly positive feeling about the brand.
Competitive advantage	A business is said to have a competitive advantage when its unique strengths, often based on cost, quality, time, and innovation, offer consumers a greater percieved value and there by diffetiating it from its competitors.
Core competency	A company's core competency are things that a firm can (alsosns) do well and that meet the following three conditions. 1. It provides customer benefits, 2. It is hard for competitors to imitate, and 3. it can be leveraged widely to many products and market. A core competency can take various forms, including technical/subject matter knowhow, a reliable process, and/or close relationships with customers and suppliers. It may also include product development or culture such as employee dedication. Modern business theories suggest that most activities that are not part of a company's core competency should be outsourced.
Core	A core is the set of feasible allocations in an economy that cannot be improved upon by subset of the set of the economy's consumers (a coalition). In construction, when the force in an element is within a certain center section, the core, the element will only be under compression.
Tangible	Having a physical existence is referred to as the tangible. Personal property other than real estate, such as cars, boats, stocks, or other assets.
Brand	A name, symbol, or design that identifies the goods or services of one seller or group of sellers and distinguishes them from the goods and services of competitors is a brand.
Configuration	An organization's shape, which reflects the division of labor and the means of coordinating the divided tasks is configuration.
Open market	In economics, the open market is the term used to refer to the environment in which bonds are bought and sold.
Facilitation	Facilitation refers to helping a team or individual achieve a goal. Often used in meetings or with teams to help the teams achieve their objectives.
Comprehensive	A comprehensive refers to a layout accurate in size, color, scheme, and other necessary details to show how a final ad will look. For presentation only, never for reproduction.

Go to **Cram101.com** for the Practice Tests for this Chapter.

Corporation	A legal entity chartered by a state or the Federal government that is distinct and separate from the individuals who own it is a corporation. This separation gives the corporation unique powers which other legal entities lack.
Contribution	In business organization law, the cash or property contributed to a business by its owners is referred to as contribution.
Gap	In December of 1995, Gap became the first major North American retailer to accept independent monitoring of the working conditions in a contract factory producing its garments. Gap is the largest specialty retailer in the United States.
Turnover	Turnover in a financial context refers to the rate at which a provider of goods cycles through its average inventory. Turnover in a human resources context refers to the characteristic of a given company or industry, relative to rate at which an employer gains and loses staff.
Peak	Peak refers to the point in the business cycle when an economic expansion reaches its highest point before turning down. Contrasts with trough.
Quality assurance	Those activities associated with assuring the quality of a product or service is called quality assurance.
Quality control	The measurement of products and services against set standards is referred to as quality control.
Analyst	Analyst refers to a person or tool with a primary function of information analysis, generally with a more limited, practical and short term set of goals than a researcher.
Subculture	A subgroups within the larger, or national, culture with unique values, ideas, and attitudes is a subculture.
Culture gap	The difference between an organization's desired cultural norms and values and actual norms and values is called culture gap.
Proactive	To be proactive is to act before a situation becomes a source of confrontation or crisis. It is the opposite of "retroactive," which refers to actions taken after an event.
Matching	Matching refers to an accounting concept that establishes when expenses are recognized. Expenses are matched with the revenues they helped to generate and are recognized when those revenues are recognized.
Allocate	Allocate refers to the assignment of income for various tax purposes. A multistate corporation's nonbusiness income usually is distributed to the state where the nonbusiness assets are located; it is not apportioned with the rest of the entity's income.
Restructuring	Restructuring is the corporate management term for the act of partially dismantling and reorganizing a company for the purpose of making it more efficient and therefore more profitable.
Swap	In finance a swap is a derivative, where two counterparties exchange one stream of cash flows against another stream. These streams are called the legs of the swap. The cash flows are calculated over a notional principal amount. Swaps are often used to hedge certain risks, for instance interest rate risk. Another use is speculation.
Consequential	Damages that do not flow directly and immediately from an act but rather flow from the results of the act are consequential.
Leverage	Leverage is using given resources in such a way that the potential positive or negative outcome is magnified. In finance, this generally refers to borrowing.
Technological	The introduction of new methods of production or new products intended to increase the

147

change	productivity of existing inputs or to raise marginal products is a technological change.
Partnership	In the common law, a partnership is a type of business entity in which partners share with each other the profits or losses of the business undertaking in which they have all invested.
Intervention	Intervention refers to an activity in which a government buys or sells its currency in the foreign exchange market in order to affect its currency's exchange rate.
Performance improvement	Performance improvement is the concept of measuring the output of a particular process or procedure then modifying the process or procedure in order to increase the output, increase efficiency, or increase the effectiveness of the process or procedure.
Performance target	A task established for an employee that provides the comparative basis for performance appraisal is a performance target.
Demand management	The use of fiscal policy and monetary policy to increase or decrease aggregate demand is called demand management.
Channel	Channel, in communications (sometimes called communications channel), refers to the medium used to convey information from a sender (or transmitter) to a receiver.
Principal	In agency law, one under whose direction an agent acts and for whose benefit that agent acts is a principal.
Subsidiary	A company that is controlled by another company or corporation is a subsidiary.
Mortgage	Mortgage refers to a note payable issued for property, such as a house, usually repaid in equal installments consisting of part principle and part interest, over a specified period.
Foundation	A Foundation is a type of philanthropic organization set up by either individuals or institutions as a legal entity (either as a corporation or trust) with the purpose of distributing grants to support causes in line with the goals of the foundation.
Corporate level	Corporate level refers to level at which top management directs overall strategy for the entire organization.
Devise	In a will, a gift of real property is called a devise.
Extension	Extension refers to an out-of-court settlement in which creditors agree to allow the firm more time to meet its financial obligations. A new repayment schedule will be developed, subject to the acceptance of creditors.
General manager	A manager who is responsible for several departments that perform different functions is called general manager.
Journal	Book of original entry, in which transactions are recorded in a general ledger system, is referred to as a journal.
Competitiveness	Competitiveness usually refers to characteristics that permit a firm to compete effectively with other firms due to low cost or superior technology, perhaps internationally.
Business value	Business value is an informal term that includes all forms of value that determine the health and well-being of the firm in the long-run.
Information technology management	Information technology management is a common business function within corporations. Strictly speaking, there are two incarnations to this definition. One implies the management of a collection of systems, infrastructure, and information that resides on them. Another implies the management of information technologies as a business function.
Management information system	A computer-based system that provides information and support for effective managerial decision makin is referred to as a management information system.

Consideration	Consideration in contract law, a basic requirement for an enforceable agreement under traditional contract principles, defined in this text as legal value, bargained for and given in exchange for an act or promise. In corporation law, cash or property contributed to a corporation in exchange for shares, or a promise to contribute such cash or property.
Business Week	Business Week is a business magazine published by McGraw-Hill. It was first published in 1929 under the direction of Malcolm Muir, who was serving as president of the McGraw-Hill Publishing company at the time. It is considered to be the standard both in industry and among students.
Enterprise resource planning	Computer-based production and operations system that links multiple firms into one integrated production unit is enterprise resource planning.
Strategic fit	In business planning, the strategic fit is an indication of how well a company's mission and strategies fit its internal capabilities and its external environment.
Research report	A research report is a business report produced by business research firms by their financial analysts. They are designed to dig out the important pieces of companies operational and financial reporting to paint a picture of the future of companies to assist debt and equity investing.
Commerce	Commerce is the exchange of something of value between two entities. It is the central mechanism from which capitalism is derived.
Evaluation	The consumer's appraisal of the product or brand on important attributes is called evaluation.

Information technology	Information technology refers to technology that helps companies change business by allowing them to use new methods.
Technology	The body of knowledge and techniques that can be used to combine economic resources to produce goods and services is called technology.
Management	Management characterizes the process of leading and directing all or part of an organization, often a business, through the deployment and manipulation of resources. Early twentieth-century management writer Mary Parker Follett defined management as "the art of getting things done through people."
Information system	An information system is a system whether automated or manual, that comprises people, machines, and/or methods organized to collect, process, transmit, and disseminate data that represent user information.
Value creation	Value creation refers to performing activities that increase the value of goods or services to consumers.
Journal	Book of original entry, in which transactions are recorded in a general ledger system, is referred to as a journal.
Business value	Business value is an informal term that includes all forms of value that determine the health and well-being of the firm in the long-run.
Strategy formulation	The process of deciding on a strategic direction by defining a company's mission and goals, its external opportunities and threats, and its internal strengths and weaknesses is referred to as a strategy formulation.
Outsourcing	Outsourcing refers to a production activity that was previously done inside a firm or plant that is now conducted outside that firm or plant.
Vendor	A person who sells property to a vendee is a vendor. The words vendor and vendee are more commonly applied to the seller and purchaser of real estate, and the words seller and buyer are more commonly applied to the seller and purchaser of personal property.
Gap	In December of 1995, Gap became the first major North American retailer to accept independent monitoring of the working conditions in a contract factory producing its garments. Gap is the largest specialty retailer in the United States.
Partnership	In the common law, a partnership is a type of business entity in which partners share with each other the profits or losses of the business undertaking in which they have all invested.
Revenue	Revenue is a U.S. business term for the amount of money that a company receives from its activities, mostly from sales of products and/or services to customers.
Marketing	Promoting and selling products or services to customers, or prospective customers, is referred to as marketing.
Investment	Investment refers to spending for the production and accumulation of capital and additions to inventories. In a financial sense, buying an asset with the expectation of making a return.
Portfolio	In finance, a portfolio is a collection of investments held by an institution or a private individual. Holding but not always a portfolio is part of an investment and risk-limiting strategy called diversification. By owning several assets, certain types of risk (in particular specific risk) can be reduced.
Research and development	The use of resources for the deliberate discovery of new information and ways of doing things, together with the application of that information in inventing new products or processes is referred to as research and development.
Advertising	Advertising refers to paid, nonpersonal communication through various media by organizations

	and individuals who are in some way identified in the advertising message.
Policy	Similar to a script in that a policy can be a less than completely rational decision-making method. Involves the use of a pre-existing set of decision steps for any problem that presents itself.
Fund	Independent accounting entity with a self-balancing set of accounts segregated for the purposes of carrying on specific activities is referred to as a fund.
Fixed cost	The cost that a firm bears if it does not produce at all and that is independent of its output. The presence of a fixed cost tends to imply increasing returns to scale. Contrasts with variable cost.
Capital	Capital generally refers to financial wealth, especially that used to start or maintain a business. In classical economics, capital is one of four factors of production, the others being land and labor and entrepreneurship.
Evaluation	The consumer's appraisal of the product or brand on important attributes is called evaluation.
Contribution	In business organization law, the cash or property contributed to a business by its owners is referred to as contribution.
Financial analysis	Financial analysis is the analysis of the accounts and the economic prospects of a firm.
Corporation	A legal entity chartered by a state or the Federal government that is distinct and separate from the individuals who own it is a corporation. This separation gives the corporation unique powers which other legal entities lack.
Assessment	Collecting information and providing feedback to employees about their behavior, communication style, or skills is an assessment.
Return on investment	Return on investment refers to the return a businessperson gets on the money he and other owners invest in the firm; for example, a business that earned $100 on a $1,000 investment would have a ROI of 10 percent: 100 divided by 1000.
Comprehensive	A comprehensive refers to a layout accurate in size, color, scheme, and other necessary details to show how a final ad will look. For presentation only, never for reproduction.
Accounting	A system that collects and processes financial information about an organization and reports that information to decision makers is referred to as accounting.
Procurement	Procurement is the acquisition of goods or services at the best possible total cost of ownership, in the right quantity, at the right time, in the right place for the direct benefit or use of the governments, corporations, or individuals generally via, but not limited to a contract.
Service	Service refers to a "non tangible product" that is not embodied in a physical good and that typically effects some change in another product, person, or institution. Contrasts with good.
Productivity	Productivity refers to the total output of goods and services in a given period of time divided by work hours.
Enabling	Enabling refers to giving workers the education and tools they need to assume their new decision-making powers.
Market	A market is, as defined in economics, a social arrangement that allows buyers and sellers to discover information and carry out a voluntary exchange of goods or services.
Invoice	The itemized bill for a transaction, stating the nature of the transaction and its cost. In

	international trade, the invoice price is often the preferred basis for levying an ad valorem tariff.
Bad debt	In accounting and finance, bad debt is the portion of receivables that can no longer be collected, typically from accounts receivable or loans. Bad debt in accounting is considered an expense.
Acceleration	Acceleration refers to the shortening of the time for the performance of a contract or the payment of a note by the operation of some provision in the contract or note itself.
Buyer	A buyer refers to a role in the buying center with formal authority and responsibility to select the supplier and negotiate the terms of the contract.
Restructuring	Restructuring is the corporate management term for the act of partially dismantling and reorganizing a company for the purpose of making it more efficient and therefore more profitable.
Innovation	Innovation refers to the first commercially successful introduction of a new product, the use of a new method of production, or the creation of a new form of business organization.
Intranet	Intranet refers to a companywide network, closed to public access, that uses Internet-type technology. A set of communications links within one company that travel over the Internet but are closed to public access.
Portfolio approach	Portfolio approach refers to an approach to explaining exchange rates that stresses their role in changing the proportions of different currency-denominated assets in portfolios. The exchange rate adjusts to equate these proportions to desired levels.
Prototype	A prototype is built to test the function of a new design before starting production of a product.
Argument	The discussion by counsel for the respective parties of their contentions on the law and the facts of the case being tried in order to aid the jury in arriving at a correct and just conclusion is called argument.
Data warehouse	A Data warehouse is a repository of integrated information, available for queries and analysis. Data and information are extracted from heterogeneous sources as they are generated.
Competitor	Other organizations in the same industry or type of business that provide a good or service to the same set of customers is referred to as a competitor.
Warehouse	Warehouse refers to a location, often decentralized, that a firm uses to store, consolidate, age, or mix stock; house product-recall programs; or ease tax burdens.
Attrition	The practice of not hiring new employees to replace older employees who either quit or retire is referred to as attrition.
Performance improvement	Performance improvement is the concept of measuring the output of a particular process or procedure then modifying the process or procedure in order to increase the output, increase efficiency, or increase the effectiveness of the process or procedure.
Core business	The core business of an organization is an idealized construct intended to express that organization's "main" or "essential" activity.
Core	A core is the set of feasible allocations in an economy that cannot be improved upon by subset of the set of the economy's consumers (a coalition). In construction, when the force in an element is within a certain center section, the core, the element will only be under compression.
Critical	Critical Success Factor is a business term for an element which is necessary for an

Go to **Cram101.com** for the Practice Tests for this Chapter.

success factor	organization or project to achieve its mission.
Success factor	The term success factor refers to the characteristics necessary for high performance; knowledge, skills, abilities, behaviors.
Monopoly	A monopoly is defined as a persistent market situation where there is only one provider of a kind of product or service.
Business unit	The lowest level of the company which contains the set of functions that carry a product through its life span from concept through manufacture, distribution, sales and service is a business unit.
Competitive disadvantage	A situation in which a firm is not implementing using strategies that are being used by competing organizations is competitive disadvantage.
Business strategy	Business strategy, which refers to the aggregated operational strategies of single business firm or that of an SBU in a diversified corporation refers to the way in which a firm competes in its chosen arenas.
Central planning	The guidance of the economy by direct government control over a large portion of economic activity, as contrasted with allowing markets to serve this purpose is called central planning.
Management team	A management team is directly responsible for managing the day-to-day operations (and profitability) of a company.
Optimum	Optimum refers to the best. Usually refers to a most preferred choice by consumers subject to a budget constraint or a profit maximizing choice by firms or industry subject to a technological constraint.
Financial control	A process in which a firm periodically compares its actual revenues, costs, and expenses with its projected ones is called financial control.
Budget	Budget refers to an account, usually for a year, of the planned expenditures and the expected receipts of an entity. For a government, the receipts are tax revenues.
Bureaucracy	Bureaucracy refers to an organization with many layers of managers who set rules and regulations and oversee all decisions.
Balance	In banking and accountancy, the outstanding balance is the amount of money owned, (or due), that remains in a deposit account (or a loan account) at a given date, after all past remittances, payments and withdrawal have been accounted for. It can be positive (then, in the balance sheet of a firm, it is an asset) or negative (a liability).
Practical approach	The approach to decision-making that combines the steps of the rational approach with the conditions in the behavioral approach to create a more realistic process for making decisions in organizations is referred to as practical approach.
Acquisition	A company's purchase of the property and obligations of another company is an acquisition.
Strategic management	A philosophy of management that links strategic planning with dayto-day decision making. Strategic management seeks a fit between an organization's external and internal environments.
Financial risk	The risk related to the inability of the firm to meet its debt obligations as they come due is called financial risk.
Decision matrix	A decision matrix is a tool used to evaluate problems, solutions, or ideas. The possibilities are listed down the left-hand side of the matrix and relevant criteria are listed across the top. Each possibility is then rated on a numeric scale of importance or effectiveness (e.g. on a scale of 1 to 10) for each criterion, and each rating is recorded in the appropriate

Go to **Cram101.com** for the Practice Tests for this Chapter.

Go to **Cram101.com** for the Practice Tests for this Chapter.
And, **NEVER** highlight a book again!

Option	A contract that gives the purchaser the option to buy or sell the underlying financial instrument at a specified price, called the exercise price or strike price, within a specific period of time.
Committee	A long-lasting, sometimes permanent team in the organization structure created to deal with tasks that recur regularly is the committee.
Rationalization	Rationalization in economics is an attempt to change a pre-existing ad-hoc workflow into one that is based on a set of published rules.
Economics	The social science dealing with the use of scarce resources to obtain the maximum satisfaction of society's virtually unlimited economic wants is an economics.
Aid	Assistance provided by countries and by international institutions such as the World Bank to developing countries in the form of monetary grants, loans at low interest rates, in kind, or a combination of these is called aid. Aid can also refer to assistance of any type rendered to benefit some group or individual.
Scope	Scope of a project is the sum total of all projects products and their requirements or features.
Senior executive	Senior executive means a chief executive officer, chief operating officer, chief financial officer and anyone in charge of a principal business unit or function.
Industry	A group of firms that produce identical or similar products is an industry. It is also used specifically to refer to an area of economic production focused on manufacturing which involves large amounts of capital investment before any profit can be realized, also called "heavy industry".
Senior management	Senior management is generally a team of individuals at the highest level of organizational management who have the day-to-day responsibilities of managing a corporation.
Change management	Change management is the process of developing a planned approach to change in an organization. Typically the objective is to maximize the collective benefits for all people involved in the change and minimize the risk of failure of implementing the change.
Context	The effect of the background under which a message often takes on more and richer meaning is a context. Context is especially important in cross-cultural interactions because some cultures are said to be high context or low context.
Best practice	Best practice is a management idea which asserts that there is a technique, method, process, activity, incentive or reward that is more effective at delivering a particular outcome than any other technique, method, process, etc.
Performance requirement	Performance requirement refers to a requirement that an importer or exporter achieve some level of performance, in terms of exporting, domestic content, etc., in order to obtain an import or export license.
Project management	Project management is the discipline of organizing and managing resources in such a way that these resources deliver all the work required to complete a project within defined scope, time, and cost constraints.
Project manager	Project manager refers to a manager responsible for a temporary work project that involves the participation of other people from various functions and levels of the organization.
Business case	The business case addresses, at a high level, the business need that a project seeks to resolve. It includes the reasons for the project, the expected business benefits, the options considered (with reasons for rejecting or carrying forward each option), the expected costs of the project, a gap analysis and the expected risks.
Inputs	The inputs used by a firm or an economy are the labor, raw materials, electricity and other

Go to **Cram101.com** for the Practice Tests for this Chapter.

resources it uses to produce its outputs.

Business process	Business process refers to the individual activities of an enterprise. Processes can be viewed at a high level, for example, 'marketing,' or at the level of detailed subprocesses, for example, 'customer retention.'.
Stakeholder	A stakeholder is an individual or group with a vested interest in or expectation for organizational performance. Usually stakeholders can either have an effect on or are affected by an organization.
Organizational performance	Organizational performance comprises the actual output or results of an organization as measured against its intended outputs (or goals and objectives).
Organizational development	The application of behavioral science knowledge in a longrange effort to improve an organization's ability to cope with change in its external environment and increase its problem-solving capabilities is referred to as organizational development.
Total quality management	The broad set of management and control processes designed to focus an entire organization and all of its employees on providing products or services that do the best possible job of satisfying the customer is called total quality management.
Management philosophy	Management philosophy refers to a philosophy that links key goal-related issues with key collaboration issues to come up with general ways by which the firm will manage its affairs.
Quality management	Quality management is a method for ensuring that all the activities necessary to design, develop and implement a product or service are effective and efficient with respect to the system and its performance.
Customer service	The ability of logistics management to satisfy users in terms of time, dependability, communication, and convenience is called the customer service.
Administration	Administration refers to the management and direction of the affairs of governments and institutions; a collective term for all policymaking officials of a government; the execution and implementation of public policy.
Gain	In finance, gain is a profit or an increase in value of an investment such as a stock or bond. Gain is calculated by fair market value or the proceeds from the sale of the investment minus the sum of the purchase price and all costs associated with it.
Quality control	The measurement of products and services against set standards is referred to as quality control.
Control system	A control system is a device or set of devices that manage the behavior of other devices. Some devices or systems are not controllable.A control system is an interconnection of components connected or related in such a manner as to command, direct, or regulate itself or another system.
Automation	Automation allows machines to do work previously accomplished by people.
Stock	In financial terminology, stock is the capital raized by a corporation, through the issuance and sale of shares.
Customer satisfaction	Customer satisfaction is a business term which is used to capture the idea of measuring how satisfied an enterprise's customers are with the organization's efforts in a marketplace.
Realization	Realization is the sale of assets when an entity is being liquidated.
Operation	A standardized method or technique that is performed repetitively, often on different materials resulting in different finished goods is called an operation.
Incentive	An incentive is any factor (financial or non-financial) that provides a motive for a particular course of action, or counts as a reason for preferring one choice to the

alternatives.

Adverse impact	Adverse impact refers to the rejection for employment, placement, or promotion of a significantly higher percentage of a protected class, when compared with a non-protected class.
Expert system	Computer systems incorporating the decision rules of people recognized as experts in a certain area are refered to as an expert system.
Configuration	An organization's shape, which reflects the division of labor and the means of coordinating the divided tasks is configuration.
Positioning	The art and science of fitting the product or service to one or more segments of the market in such a way as to set it meaningfully apart from competition is called positioning.
Action plan	Action plan refers to a written document that includes the steps the trainee and manager will take to ensure that training transfers to the job.
Unit cost	Unit cost refers to cost computed by dividing some amount of total costs by the related number of units. Also called average cost.
Project plan	A project plan lists the amount of time and the budget needed to complete the tasks involved in a project.
Deliverable	A deliverable refers to a product created as a result of project work.
Systems design	Systems design is the process or art of defining the hardware and software architecture, components, modules, interfaces, and data for a computer system to satisfy specified requirements.
Business development	Business development emcompasses a number of techniques designed to grow an economic enterprise. Such techniques include, but are not limited to, assessments of marketing opportunities and target markets, intelligence gathering on customers and competitors, generating leads for possible sales, followup sales activity, and formal proposal writing.
Users	Users refer to people in the organization who actually use the product or service purchased by the buying center.
Abandonment	Abandonment in law, is the relinquishment of an interest, claim, privilege or possession. This broad meaning has a number of applications in different branches of law.
Stock exchange	A stock exchange is a corporation or mutual organization which provides facilities for stock brokers and traders, to trade company stocks and other securities.
Exchange	The trade of things of value between buyer and seller so that each is better off after the trade is called the exchange.
Pension	A pension is a steady income given to a person (usually after retirement). Pensions are typically payments made in the form of a guaranteed annuity to a retired or disabled employee.
Action research	The process of systematically collecting data on an organization, feeding it back for action planning, and evaluating results by collecting and reflecting on more data is referred to as action research.
Regulation	Regulation refers to restrictions state and federal laws place on business with regard to the conduct of its activities.
Strategic planning	The process of determining the major goals of the organization and the policies and strategies for obtaining and using resources to achieve those goals is called strategic planning.

Go to **Cram101.com** for the Practice Tests for this Chapter.

Matching	Matching refers to an accounting concept that establishes when expenses are recognized. Expenses are matched with the revenues they helped to generate and are recognized when those revenues are recognized.
Profit	Profit refers to the return to the resource entrepreneurial ability; total revenue minus total cost.
Bond	Bond refers to a debt instrument, issued by a borrower and promising a specified stream of payments to the purchaser, usually regular interest payments plus a final repayment of principal.
Business transformation	Business transformation is a key executive management initiative that attempts to align the technology initiatives of a company more closely with its business strategy and vision. Business transformation is achieved through efforts from the business and IT sides of the company.
Management information system	A computer-based system that provides information and support for effective managerial decision makin is referred to as a management information system.
Information technology management	Information technology management is a common business function within corporations. Strictly speaking, there are two incarnations to this definition. One implies the management of a collection of systems, infrastructure, and information that resides on them. Another implies the management of information technologies as a business function.
Competitive advantage	A business is said to have a competitive advantage when its unique strengths, often based on cost, quality, time, and innovation, offer consumers a greater percieved value and there by diffetiating it from its competitors.
Case study	A case study is a particular method of qualitative research. Rather than using large samples and following a rigid protocol to examine a limited number of variables, case study methods involve an in-depth, longitudinal examination of a single instance or event: a case. They provide a systematic way of looking at events, collecting data, analyzing information, and reporting the results.
Harvard Business Review	Harvard Business Review is a research-based magazine written for business practitioners, it claims a high ranking business readership and enjoys the reverence of academics, executives, and management consultants. It has been the frequent publishing home for well known scholars and management thinkers.

Go to **Cram101.com** for the Practice Tests for this Chapter.

Information technology	Information technology refers to technology that helps companies change business by allowing them to use new methods.
Information system	An information system is a system whether automated or manual, that comprises people, machines, and/or methods organized to collect, process, transmit, and disseminate data that represent user information.
Best practice	Best practice is a management idea which asserts that there is a technique, method, process, activity, incentive or reward that is more effective at delivering a particular outcome than any other technique, method, process, etc.
Productivity	Productivity refers to the total output of goods and services in a given period of time divided by work hours.
Assessment	Collecting information and providing feedback to employees about their behavior, communication style, or skills is an assessment.
Case study	A case study is a particular method of qualitative research. Rather than using large samples and following a rigid protocol to examine a limited number of variables, case study methods involve an in-depth, longitudinal examination of a single instance or event: a case. They provide a systematic way of looking at events, collecting data, analyzing information, and reporting the results.
Technology	The body of knowledge and techniques that can be used to combine economic resources to produce goods and services is called technology.
Management	Management characterizes the process of leading and directing all or part of an organization, often a business, through the deployment and manipulation of resources. Early twentieth-century management writer Mary Parker Follett defined management as "the art of getting things done through people."
Paradox	As used in economics, paradox means something unexpected, rather than the more extreme normal meaning of something seemingly impossible. Some paradoxes are just theoretical results that go against what one thinks of as normal.
Financial market	In economics, a financial market is a mechanism which allows people to trade money for securities or commodities such as gold or other precious metals. In general, any commodity market might be considered to be a financial market, if the usual purpose of traders is not the immediate consumption of the commodity, but rather as a means of delaying or accelerating consumption over time.
Investment	Investment refers to spending for the production and accumulation of capital and additions to inventories. In a financial sense, buying an asset with the expectation of making a return.
Market	A market is, as defined in economics, a social arrangement that allows buyers and sellers to discover information and carry out a voluntary exchange of goods or services.
Management information system	A computer-based system that provides information and support for effective managerial decision makin is referred to as a management information system.
Journal	Book of original entry, in which transactions are recorded in a general ledger system, is referred to as a journal.
Project management	Project management is the discipline of organizing and managing resources in such a way that these resources deliver all the work required to complete a project within defined scope, time, and cost constraints.
Escalation	Regarding the structure of tariffs. In the context of a trade war, escalation refers to the increase in tariffs that occurs as countries retaliate again and again.

Abandonment	Abandonment in law, is the relinquishment of an interest, claim, privilege or possession. This broad meaning has a number of applications in different branches of law.
Knowledge management	Sharing, organizing and disseminating information in the simplest and most relevant way possible for the users of the information is a knowledge management.
Evaluation	The consumer's appraisal of the product or brand on important attributes is called evaluation.
Portfolio	In finance, a portfolio is a collection of investments held by an institution or a private individual. Holding but not always a portfolio is part of an investment and risk-limiting strategy called diversification. By owning several assets, certain types of risk (in particular specific risk) can be reduced.
Raw material	Raw material refers to a good that has not been transformed by production; a primary product.
Context	The effect of the background under which a message often takes on more and richer meaning is a context. Context is especially important in cross-cultural interactions because some cultures are said to be high context or low context.
Innovation	Innovation refers to the first commercially successful introduction of a new product, the use of a new method of production, or the creation of a new form of business organization.
Explicit knowledge	Explicit knowledge is knowledge that has been or can be articulated, codified, and stored in certain media. The most common forms of explicit knowledge are manuals, documents, procedures, and stories. Knowledge also can be audio-visual.
Chief information officer	The chief information officer is a job title for the head of information technology group within an organization. They often report to the chief executive officer or chief financial officer.
Senior management	Senior management is generally a team of individuals at the highest level of organizational management who have the day-to-day responsibilities of managing a corporation.
Competitiveness	Competitiveness usually refers to characteristics that permit a firm to compete effectively with other firms due to low cost or superior technology, perhaps internationally.
Asset	An item of property, such as land, capital, money, a share in ownership, or a claim on others for future payment, such as a bond or a bank deposit is an asset.
Comprehensive	A comprehensive refers to a layout accurate in size, color, scheme, and other necessary details to show how a final ad will look. For presentation only, never for reproduction.
Policy	Similar to a script in that a policy can be a less than completely rational decision-making method. Involves the use of a pre-existing set of decision steps for any problem that presents itself.
Users	Users refer to people in the organization who actually use the product or service purchased by the buying center.
Acquisition	A company's purchase of the property and obligations of another company is an acquisition.
Promotion	Promotion refers to all the techniques sellers use to motivate people to buy products or services. An attempt by marketers to inform people about products and to persuade them to participate in an exchange.
Complexity	The technical sophistication of the product and hence the amount of understanding required to use it is referred to as complexity. It is the opposite of simplicity.
Production	The creation of finished goods and services using the factors of production: land, labor, capital, entrepreneurship, and knowledge.

Manufacturing	Production of goods primarily by the application of labor and capital to raw materials and other intermediate inputs, in contrast to agriculture, mining, forestry, fishing, and services a manufacturing.
Management system	A management system is the framework of processes and procedures used to ensure that an organization can fulfill all tasks required to achieve its objectives.
Business strategy	Business strategy, which refers to the aggregated operational strategies of single business firm or that of an SBU in a diversified corporation refers to the way in which a firm competes in its chosen arenas.
Quality control	The measurement of products and services against set standards is referred to as quality control.
Integration	Economic integration refers to reducing barriers among countries to transactions and to movements of goods, capital, and labor, including harmonization of laws, regulations, and standards. Integrated markets theoretically function as a unified market.
Proprietary	Proprietary indicates that a party, or proprietor, exercises private ownership, control or use over an item of property, usually to the exclusion of other parties. Where a party, holds or claims proprietary interests in relation to certain types of property (eg. a creative literary work, or software), that property may also be the subject of intellectual property law (eg. copyright or patents).
Intranet	Intranet refers to a companywide network, closed to public access, that uses Internet-type technology. A set of communications links within one company that travel over the Internet but are closed to public access.
Exchange	The trade of things of value between buyer and seller so that each is better off after the trade is called the exchange.
Board of directors	The group of individuals elected by the stockholders of a corporation to oversee its operations is a board of directors.
Committee	A long-lasting, sometimes permanent team in the organization structure created to deal with tasks that recur regularly is the committee.
Incentive	An incentive is any factor (financial or non-financial) that provides a motive for a particular course of action, or counts as a reason for preferring one choice to the alternatives.
Compliance	A type of influence process where a receiver accepts the position advocated by a source to obtain favorable outcomes or to avoid punishment is the compliance.
Alignment	Term that refers to optimal coordination among disparate departments and divisions within a firm is referred to as alignment.
Drucker	Drucker as a business thinker took off in the 1940s, when his initial writings on politics and society won him access to the internal workings of General Motors, which was one of the largest companies in the world at that time. His experiences in Europe had left him fascinated with the problem of authority.
Public utility	A firm that produces an essential good or service, has obtained from a government the right to be the sole supplier of the good or service in the area, and is regulated by that government to prevent the abuse of its monopoly power is a public utility.
Utility	Utility refers to the want-satisfying power of a good or service; the satisfaction or pleasure a consumer obtains from the consumption of a good or service.
Enabling	Enabling refers to giving workers the education and tools they need to assume their new decision-making powers.

Enterprise	Enterprise refers to another name for a business organization. Other similar terms are business firm, sometimes simply business, sometimes simply firm, as well as company, and entity.
Core business	The core business of an organization is an idealized construct intended to express that organization's "main" or "essential" activity.
Core	A core is the set of feasible allocations in an economy that cannot be improved upon by subset of the set of the economy's consumers (a coalition). In construction, when the force in an element is within a certain center section, the core, the element will only be under compression.
Value chain	The sequence of business functions in which usefulness is added to the products or services of a company is a value chain.
Confirmed	When the seller's bank agrees to assume liability on the letter of credit issued by the buyer's bank the transaction is confirmed. The term means that the credit is not only backed up by the issuing foreign bank, but that payment is also guaranteed by the notifying American bank.
Business process	Business process refers to the individual activities of an enterprise. Processes can be viewed at a high level, for example, 'marketing,' or at the level of detailed subprocesses, for example, 'customer retention.'.
Business value	Business value is an informal term that includes all forms of value that determine the health and well-being of the firm in the long-run.
Specialist	A specialist is a trader who makes a market in one or several stocks and holds the limit order book for those stocks.
Revenue	Revenue is a U.S. business term for the amount of money that a company receives from its activities, mostly from sales of products and/or services to customers.
Contribution	In business organization law, the cash or property contributed to a business by its owners is referred to as contribution.
Administration	Administration refers to the management and direction of the affairs of governments and institutions; a collective term for all policymaking officials of a government; the execution and implementation of public policy.
Prototype	A prototype is built to test the function of a new design before starting production of a product.
Warrant	A warrant is a security that entitles the holder to buy or sell a certain additional quantity of an underlying security at an agreed-upon price, at the holder's discretion.
Driving force	The key external pressure that will shape the future for an organization is a driving force. The driving force in an industry are the main underlying causes of changing industry and competitive conditions.
Marketing	Promoting and selling products or services to customers, or prospective customers, is referred to as marketing.
Targeting	In advertizing, targeting is to select a demographic or other group of people to advertise to, and create advertisements appropriately.
Customer satisfaction	Customer satisfaction is a business term which is used to capture the idea of measuring how satisfied an enterprise's customers are with the organization's efforts in a marketplace.
Extension	Extension refers to an out-of-court settlement in which creditors agree to allow the firm more time to meet its financial obligations. A new repayment schedule will be developed,

	subject to the acceptance of creditors.
Service	Service refers to a "non tangible product" that is not embodied in a physical good and that typically effects some change in another product, person, or institution. Contrasts with good.
Trial	An examination before a competent tribunal, according to the law of the land, of the facts or law put in issue in a cause, for the purpose of determining such issue is a trial. When the court hears and determines any issue of fact or law for the purpose of determining the rights of the parties, it may be considered a trial.
Supply	Supply is the aggregate amount of any material good that can be called into being at a certain price point; it comprises one half of the equation of supply and demand. In classical economic theory, a curve representing supply is one of the factors that produce price.
Reverse engineering	Reverse engineering refers to the process of learning how a product is made by taking it apart and examining it.
Argument	The discussion by counsel for the respective parties of their contentions on the law and the facts of the case being tried in order to aid the jury in arriving at a correct and just conclusion is called argument.
Knowledge worker	Employees who own the means of producing a product or service are called a knowledge worker.
Bad debt	In accounting and finance, bad debt is the portion of receivables that can no longer be collected, typically from accounts receivable or loans. Bad debt in accounting is considered an expense.
Channel	Channel, in communications (sometimes called communications channel), refers to the medium used to convey information from a sender (or transmitter) to a receiver.
Brief	Brief refers to a statement of a party's case or legal arguments, usually prepared by an attorney. Also used to make legal arguments before appellate courts.
Business model	A business model is the instrument by which a business intends to generate revenue and profits. It is a summary of how a company means to serve its employees and customers, and involves both strategy (what an business intends to do) as well as an implementation.
Competitive advantage	A business is said to have a competitive advantage when its unique strengths, often based on cost, quality, time, and innovation, offer consumers a greater percieved value and there by differtiating it from its competitors.
Logistics	Those activities that focus on getting the right amount of the right products to the right place at the right time at the lowest possible cost is referred to as logistics.
Consideration	Consideration in contract law, a basic requirement for an enforceable agreement under traditional contract principles, defined in this text as legal value, bargained for and given in exchange for an act or promise. In corporation law, cash or property contributed to a corporation in exchange for shares, or a promise to contribute such cash or property.
Business risk	The risk related to the inability of the firm to hold its competitive position and maintain stability and growth in earnings is business risk.
Database management system	A database management system is a computer program (or more typically, a suite of them) designed to manage a database (a large set of structured data), and run operations on the data requested by numerous clients.
Distribution	Distribution in economics, the manner in which total output and income is distributed among individuals or factors.
Trust	An arrangement in which shareholders of independent firms agree to give up their stock in

exchange for trust certificates that entitle them to a share of the trust's common profits.

Customer database	Customer database refers to a computer database specifically designed for storage, retrieval, and analysis of customer data by marketers.
Asset management	Asset management is the method that a company uses to track fixed assets, for example factory equipment, desks and chairs, computers, even buildings. Although the exact details of the task varies widely from company to company, asset management often includes tracking the physical location of assets, managing demand for scarce resources, and accounting tasks such as amortization.
Scope	Scope of a project is the sum total of all projects products and their requirements or features.
Resource management	Resource management is the efficient and effective deployment of an organization's resources when they are needed. Such resources may include financial resources, inventory, human skills, production resources, or information technology.
Competitor	Other organizations in the same industry or type of business that provide a good or service to the same set of customers is referred to as a competitor.
Buyer	A buyer refers to a role in the buying center with formal authority and responsibility to select the supplier and negotiate the terms of the contract.
Business unit	The lowest level of the company which contains the set of functions that carry a product through its life span from concept through manufacture, distribution, sales and service is a business unit.
Collaboration	Collaboration occurs when the interaction between groups is very important to goal attainment and the goals are compatible. Wherein people work together —applying both to the work of individuals as well as larger collectives and societies.
Decentralization	Decentralization is the process of redistributing decision-making closer to the point of service or action. This gives freedom to managers at lower levels of the organization to make decisions.
Centralization	A structural policy in which decision-making authority is concentrated at the top of the organizational hierarchy is referred to as centralization.
Protocol	Protocol refers to a statement that, before product development begins, identifies a well-defined target market; specific customers' needs, wants, and preferences; and what the product will be and do.
Vendor	A person who sells property to a vendee is a vendor. The words vendor and vendee are more commonly applied to the seller and purchaser of real estate, and the words seller and buyer are more commonly applied to the seller and purchaser of personal property.
Return on investment	Return on investment refers to the return a businessperson gets on the money he and other owners invest in the firm; for example, a business that earned $100 on a $1,000 investment would have a ROI of 10 percent: 100 divided by 1000.
Strategic business unit	Strategic business unit is understood as a business unit within the overall corporate identity which is distinguishable from other business because it serves a defined external market where management can conduct strategic planning in relation to products and markets. When companies become really large, they are best thought of as being composed of a number of businesses
Configuration	An organization's shape, which reflects the division of labor and the means of coordinating the divided tasks is configuration.
Warehouse	Warehouse refers to a location, often decentralized, that a firm uses to store, consolidate,

Go to **Cram101.com** for the Practice Tests for this Chapter.

age, or mix stock; house product-recall programs; or ease tax burdens.

Data warehouse	A Data warehouse is a repository of integrated information, available for queries and analysis. Data and information are extracted from heterogeneous sources as they are generated.
Preparation	Preparation refers to usually the first stage in the creative process. It includes education and formal training.
Security	Security refers to a claim on the borrower future income that is sold by the borrower to the lender. A security is a type of transferable interest representing financial value.
Principal	In agency law, one under whose direction an agent acts and for whose benefit that agent acts is a principal.
Interest	In finance and economics, interest is the price paid by a borrower for the use of a lender's money. In other words, interest is the amount of paid to "rent" money for a period of time.
Customer relationship management	Learning as much as possible about customers and doing everything you can to satisfy them or even delight them with goods and services over time is customer relationship management.
Enterprise resource planning	Computer-based production and operations system that links multiple firms into one integrated production unit is enterprise resource planning.
Relationship management	A method for developing long-term associations with customers is referred to as relationship management.
Benchmarking	The continuous process of comparing the levels of performance in producing products and services and executing activities against the best levels of performance is benchmarking.
Restructuring	Restructuring is the corporate management term for the act of partially dismantling and reorganizing a company for the purpose of making it more efficient and therefore more profitable.
Recovery	Characterized by rizing output, falling unemployment, rizing profits, and increasing economic activity following a decline is a recovery.
Gain	In finance, gain is a profit or an increase in value of an investment such as a stock or bond. Gain is calculated by fair market value or the proceeds from the sale of the investment minus the sum of the purchase price and all costs associated with it.
Authority	Authority in agency law, refers to an agent's ability to affect his principal's legal relations with third parties. Also used to refer to an actor's legal power or ability to do something. In addition, sometimes used to refer to a statute, case, or other legal source that justifies a particular result.
Continuous process	An uninterrupted production process in which long production runs turn out finished goods over time is called continuous process.
Organizational structure	Organizational structure is the way in which the interrelated groups of an organization are constructed. From a managerial point of view the main concerns are ensuring effective communication and coordination.
Administrator	Administrator refers to the personal representative appointed by a probate court to settle the estate of a deceased person who died.
Misuse	A defense that relieves a seller of product liability if the user abnormally misused the product is called misuse. Products must be designed to protect against foreseeable misuse.
Corruption	The unauthorized use of public office for private gain. The most common forms of corruption

Go to **Cram101.com** for the Practice Tests for this Chapter.

are bribery, extortion, and the misuse of inside information.

Intervention	Intervention refers to an activity in which a government buys or sells its currency in the foreign exchange market in order to affect its currency's exchange rate.
New product development	New product development is the complete process of bringing a new product to market. There are two parallel aspects to this process : one involves product engineering ; the other marketing analysis.
Product development	In business and engineering, new product development is the complete process of bringing a new product to market. There are two parallel aspects to this process : one involves product engineering ; the other marketing analysis. Marketers see new product development as the first stage in product life cycle management, engineers as part of Product Lifecycle Management.
Stock	In financial terminology, stock is the capital raized by a corporation, through the issuance and sale of shares.
Contingency planning	The process of preparing alternative courses of action that may be used if the primary plans do not achieve the objectives of the organization is called contingency planning.
Common area	Common area is area on a piece of property or part of a building that is available for use to all owners or tenents. Examples include: hallways, swimming pools, parking garage, and cummunity centers.
Learning curve	Learning curve is a function that measures how labor-hours per unit decline as units of production increase because workers are learning and becoming better at their jobs.
Economics	The social science dealing with the use of scarce resources to obtain the maximum satisfaction of society's virtually unlimited economic wants is an economics.
Preference	The act of a debtor in paying or securing one or more of his creditors in a manner more favorable to them than to other creditors or to the exclusion of such other creditors is a preference. In the absence of statute, a preference is perfectly good, but to be legal it must be bona fide, and not a mere subterfuge of the debtor to secure a future benefit to himself or to prevent the application of his property to his debts.
Supply chain	Supply chain refers to the flow of goods, services, and information from the initial sources of materials and services to the delivery of products to consumers.
Exporting	Selling products to another country is called exporting.
Bid	A bid price is a price offered by a buyer when he/she buys a good. In the context of stock trading on a stock exchange, the bid price is the highest price a buyer of a stock is willing to pay for a share of that given stock.
Business opportunity	A business opportunity involves the sale or lease of any product, service, equipment, etc. that will enable the purchaser-licensee to begin a business
Yield	The interest rate that equates a future value or an annuity to a given present value is a yield.
Physical resources	Natural resources used in the transformation process to create resources of more value are called physical resources.
Substitute product	Any product viewed by a consumer as an alternative for other products is a substitute product. The substitution is rarely perfect, and varies from time to time depending on price, availability, etc.
Globalization	The increasing world-wide integration of markets for goods, services and capital that attracted special attention in the late 1990s is called globalization.

Deregulation	The lessening or complete removal of government regulations on an industry, especially concerning the price that firms are allowed to charge and leaving price to be determined by market forces a deregulation.
Chief knowledge officer	A chief knowledge officer is an organizational leader, responsible for ensuring that the organization maximizes the value it achieves through knowledge.
Regulation	Regulation refers to restrictions state and federal laws place on business with regard to the conduct of its activities.
Customs	Customs is an authority or agency in a country responsible for collecting customs duties and for controlling the flow of people, animals and goods (including personal effects and hazardous items) in and out of the country.
Expert system	Computer systems incorporating the decision rules of people recognized as experts in a certain area are refered to as an expert system.
Ford	Ford is an American company that manufactures and sells automobiles worldwide. Ford introduced methods for large-scale manufacturing of cars, and large-scale management of an industrial workforce, especially elaborately engineered manufacturing sequences typified by the moving assembly lines.
Intellectual capital	Intellectual capital makes an organization worth more than its balance sheet value. For many years, intellectual capital and goodwill meant the same thing. Today, intellectual capital management is far broader. It seeks to explain how knowledge, collaboration, and process-engagement create decisions and actions that lead to cost allocations, productivity, and finally financial performance.
Capital	Capital generally refers to financial wealth, especially that used to start or maintain a business. In classical economics, capital is one of four factors of production, the others being land and labor and entrepreneurship.
Tacit knowledge	Knowledge that has not been articulated. Tacit knowledge is often subconscious and relatively difficult to communicate to other people. Tacit knowledge consists often of habits and culture that we do not recognize in ourselves.
Categorizing	The act of placing strengths and weaknesses into categories in generic internal assessment is called categorizing.
Indexing	Indexing refers to provisions in a law or a contract whereby monetary payments are automatically adjusted whenever a specified price index changes.
Facilitator	A facilitator is someone who skilfully helps a group of people understand their common objectives and plan to achieve them without personally taking any side of the argument.
Workflow	Workflow refers to automated systems that electronically route documents to the next person in the process.
Contract	A contract is a "promise" or an "agreement" that is enforced or recognized by the law. In the civil law, a contract is considered to be part of the general law of obligations.
Effective communication	When the intended meaning equals the perceived meaning it is called effective communication.
Xerox	Xerox was founded in 1906 as "The Haloid Company" manufacturing photographic paper and equipment. The company came to prominence in 1959 with the introduction of the first plain paper photocopier using the process of xerography (electrophotography) developed by Chester Carlson, the Xerox 914.
Business plan	A detailed written statement that describes the nature of the business, the target market, the advantages the business will have in relation to competition, and the resources and

Go to **Cram101.com** for the Practice Tests for this Chapter.

	qualifications of the owner is referred to as a business plan.
Automation	Automation allows machines to do work previously accomplished by people.
Leverage	Leverage is using given resources in such a way that the potential positive or negative outcome is magnified. In finance, this generally refers to borrowing.
Leadership	Management merely consists of leadership applied to business situations; or in other words: management forms a sub-set of the broader process of leadership.
Tangible	Having a physical existence is referred to as the tangible. Personal property other than real estate, such as cars, boats, stocks, or other assets.
Competitive intelligence	Competitive Intelligence is defined as business intelligence focusing on the external competitive environment.
Gatekeeper	Gatekeeper refers to an individual who has a strategic position in the network that allows him or her to control information moving in either direction through a channel.
Analyst	Analyst refers to a person or tool with a primary function of information analysis, generally with a more limited, practical and short term set of goals than a researcher.
Strategic alliance	Strategic alliance refers to a long-term partnership between two or more companies established to help each company build competitive market advantages.
Aggregation	Aggregation refers to the combining of two or more things into a single category. Data on international trade necessarily aggregate goods and services into manageable groups.
Balance	In banking and accountancy, the outstanding balance is the amount of money owned, (or due), that remains in a deposit account (or a loan account) at a given date, after all past remittances, payments and withdrawal have been accounted for. It can be positive (then, in the balance sheet of a firm, it is an asset) or negative (a liability).
Free market	A free market is a market where price is determined by the unregulated interchange of supply and demand rather than set by artificial means.
Monopoly	A monopoly is defined as a persistent market situation where there is only one provider of a kind of product or service.
Harvard Business Review	Harvard Business Review is a research-based magazine written for business practitioners, it claims a high ranking business readership and enjoys the reverence of academics, executives, and management consultants. It has been the frequent publishing home for well known scholars and management thinkers.
Contingency perspective	Contingency perspective suggests that, in most organizations, situations and outcomes are contingent on, or influenced by, other variables.
Bottom line	The bottom line is net income on the last line of a income statement.
Strategic management	A philosophy of management that links strategic planning with dayto-day decision making. Strategic management seeks a fit between an organization's external and internal environments.
Firm	An organization that employs resources to produce a good or service for profit and owns and operates one or more plants is referred to as a firm.
Equity	Equity is the name given to the set of legal principles, in countries following the English common law tradition, which supplement strict rules of law where their application would operate harshly, so as to achieve what is sometimes referred to as "natural justice."
Theory of the firm	The theory of the firm consists of a number of economic theories which describe the nature of the firm (company or corporation), including its behavior and its relationship with the

Go to **Cram101.com** for the Practice Tests for this Chapter.

market.

Go to **Cram101.com** for the Practice Tests for this Chapter.

Strategic management	A philosophy of management that links strategic planning with dayto-day decision making. Strategic management seeks a fit between an organization's external and internal environments.
Theory of the firm	The theory of the firm consists of a number of economic theories which describe the nature of the firm (company or corporation), including its behavior and its relationship with the market.
Management	Management characterizes the process of leading and directing all or part of an organization, often a business, through the deployment and manipulation of resources. Early twentieth-century management writer Mary Parker Follett defined management as "the art of getting things done through people."
Journal	Book of original entry, in which transactions are recorded in a general ledger system, is referred to as a journal.
Grant	Grant refers to an intergovernmental transfer of funds . Since the New Deal, state and local governments have become increasingly dependent upon federal grants for an almost infinite variety of programs.
Asset	An item of property, such as land, capital, money, a share in ownership, or a claim on others for future payment, such as a bond or a bank deposit is an asset.
Firm	An organization that employs resources to produce a good or service for profit and owns and operates one or more plants is referred to as a firm.
Integration	Economic integration refers to reducing barriers among countries to transactions and to movements of goods, capital, and labor, including harmonization of laws, regulations, and standards. Integrated markets theoretically function as a unified market.
Harvard Business Review	Harvard Business Review is a research-based magazine written for business practitioners, it claims a high ranking business readership and enjoys the reverence of academics, executives, and management consultants. It has been the frequent publishing home for well known scholars and management thinkers.
Information technology	Information technology refers to technology that helps companies change business by allowing them to use new methods.
Knowledge management	Sharing, organizing and disseminating information in the simplest and most relevant way possible for the users of the information is a knowledge management.
British Petroleum	British Petroleum, is a British energy company with headquarters in London, one of four vertically integrated private sector oil, natural gas, and petrol (gasoline) "supermajors" in the world, along with Royal Dutch Shell, ExxonMobil and Total.
Accounting	A system that collects and processes financial information about an organization and reports that information to decision makers is referred to as accounting.
Technology	The body of knowledge and techniques that can be used to combine economic resources to produce goods and services is called technology.
Xerox	Xerox was founded in 1906 as "The Haloid Company" manufacturing photographic paper and equipment. The company came to prominence in 1959 with the introduction of the first plain paper photocopier using the process of xerography (electrophotography) developed by Chester Carlson, the Xerox 914.
Information system	An information system is a system whether automated or manual, that comprises people, machines, and/or methods organized to collect, process, transmit, and disseminate data that represent user information.
Service	Service refers to a "non tangible product" that is not embodied in a physical good and that

	typically effects some change in another product, person, or institution. Contrasts with good.
Supply	Supply is the aggregate amount of any material good that can be called into being at a certain price point; it comprises one half of the equation of supply and demand. In classical economic theory, a curve representing supply is one of the factors that produce price.
Investment	Investment refers to spending for the production and accumulation of capital and additions to inventories. In a financial sense, buying an asset with the expectation of making a return.
Outsourcing	Outsourcing refers to a production activity that was previously done inside a firm or plant that is now conducted outside that firm or plant.
Consultant	A professional that provides expert advice in a particular field or area in which customers occassionaly require this type of knowledge is a consultant.
Specialist	A specialist is a trader who makes a market in one or several stocks and holds the limit order book for those stocks.
Commodity	Could refer to any good, but in trade a commodity is usually a raw material or primary product that enters into international trade, such as metals or basic agricultural products.
Buyer	A buyer refers to a role in the buying center with formal authority and responsibility to select the supplier and negotiate the terms of the contract.
Production	The creation of finished goods and services using the factors of production: land, labor, capital, entrepreneurship, and knowledge.
Operation	A standardized method or technique that is performed repetitively, often on different materials resulting in different finished goods is called an operation.
Users	Users refer to people in the organization who actually use the product or service purchased by the buying center.
Enabling	Enabling refers to giving workers the education and tools they need to assume their new decision-making powers.
Customer service	The ability of logistics management to satisfy users in terms of time, dependability, communication, and convenience is called the customer service.
Contribution	In business organization law, the cash or property contributed to a business by its owners is referred to as contribution.
Operations management	A specialized area in management that converts or transforms resources into goods and services is operations management.
Complexity	The technical sophistication of the product and hence the amount of understanding required to use it is referred to as complexity. It is the opposite of simplicity.
Budget	Budget refers to an account, usually for a year, of the planned expenditures and the expected receipts of an entity. For a government, the receipts are tax revenues.
Holder	A person in possession of a document of title or an instrument payable or indorsed to him, his order, or to bearer is a holder.
Business analysis	Business analysis is a structured methodology that is focused on completely understanding the customer's needs, identifying how best to meet those needs, and then "reinventing" the stream of processes to meet those needs.
Capacity planning	The determination and adjustment of the organization's ability to produce products and services to match customer demand is called capacity planning.
Customer contact	Customer contact refers to a characteristic of services that notes that customers tend to be

more involved in the production of services than they are in manufactured goods.

Perceived quality	A dimension of quality identified by David Garvin that refers to a subjective assessment of a product's quality based on criteria defined by the observer is a perceived quality.
Compliance	A type of influence process where a receiver accepts the position advocated by a source to obtain favorable outcomes or to avoid punishment is the compliance.
Euro	The common currency of a subset of the countries of the EU, adopted January 1, 1999 is called euro.
Performance measurement	The process by which someone evaluates an employee's work behaviors by measurement and comparison with previously established standards, documents the results, and communicates the results to the employee is called performance measurement.
Back office	A back office is a part of most corporations where tasks dedicated to running the company itself take place.
Assessment	Collecting information and providing feedback to employees about their behavior, communication style, or skills is an assessment.
Evaluation	The consumer's appraisal of the product or brand on important attributes is called evaluation.
Vendor	A person who sells property to a vendee is a vendor. The words vendor and vendee are more commonly applied to the seller and purchaser of real estate, and the words seller and buyer are more commonly applied to the seller and purchaser of personal property.
Help desk	The group in an organization that provides support for both hardware and software. The term is also used in connection with specialized software that supports help desk operations.
Matching	Matching refers to an accounting concept that establishes when expenses are recognized. Expenses are matched with the revenues they helped to generate and are recognized when those revenues are recognized.
Facilitation	Facilitation refers to helping a team or individual achieve a goal. Often used in meetings or with teams to help the teams achieve their objectives.
Deliverable	A deliverable refers to a product created as a result of project work.
Real value	Real value is the value of anything expressed in money of the day with the effects of inflation removed.
Procurement	Procurement is the acquisition of goods or services at the best possible total cost of ownership, in the right quantity, at the right time, in the right place for the direct benefit or use of the governments, corporations, or individuals generally via, but not limited to a contract.
Positioning	The art and science of fitting the product or service to one or more segments of the market in such a way as to set it meaningfully apart from competition is called positioning.
Contract	A contract is a "promise" or an "agreement" that is enforced or recognized by the law. In the civil law, a contract is considered to be part of the general law of obligations.
Option	A contract that gives the purchaser the option to buy or sell the underlying financial instrument at a specified price, called the exercise price or strike price, within a specific period of time.
Closing	The finalization of a real estate sales transaction that passes title to the property from the seller to the buyer is referred to as a closing. Closing is a sales term which refers to the process of making a sale. It refers to reaching the final step, which may be an exchange of money or acquiring a signature.

Go to **Cram101.com** for the Practice Tests for this Chapter.

Gap	In December of 1995, Gap became the first major North American retailer to accept independent monitoring of the working conditions in a contract factory producing its garments. Gap is the largest specialty retailer in the United States.
Bureaucracy	Bureaucracy refers to an organization with many layers of managers who set rules and regulations and oversee all decisions.
Standardization	Standardization, in the context related to technologies and industries, is the process of establishing a technical standard among competing entities in a market, where this will bring benefits without hurting competition.
Teamwork	That which occurs when group members work together in ways that utilize their skills well to accomplish a purpose is called teamwork.
Senior management	Senior management is generally a team of individuals at the highest level of organizational management who have the day-to-day responsibilities of managing a corporation.
Context	The effect of the background under which a message often takes on more and richer meaning is a context. Context is especially important in cross-cultural interactions because some cultures are said to be high context or low context.
Premium	Premium refers to the fee charged by an insurance company for an insurance policy. The rate of losses must be relatively predictable: In order to set the premium (prices) insurers must be able to estimate them accurately.
Industry	A group of firms that produce identical or similar products is an industry. It is also used specifically to refer to an area of economic production focused on manufacturing which involves large amounts of capital investment before any profit can be realized, also called "heavy industry".
Configuration	An organization's shape, which reflects the division of labor and the means of coordinating the divided tasks is configuration.
Incremental cost	Additional total cost incurred for an activity is called incremental cost. A form of costing that classifies costs into their fixed and variable elements in order to calculate the extra cost of making and selling an additional batch of units.
Acquisition	A company's purchase of the property and obligations of another company is an acquisition.
Competitive advantage	A business is said to have a competitive advantage when its unique strengths, often based on cost, quality, time, and innovation, offer consumers a greater percieved value and there by diffetiating it from its competitors.
Business process	Business process refers to the individual activities of an enterprise. Processes can be viewed at a high level, for example, 'marketing,' or at the level of detailed subprocesses, for example, 'customer retention.'.
Portfolio	In finance, a portfolio is a collection of investments held by an institution or a private individual. Holding but not always a portfolio is part of an investment and risk-limiting strategy called diversification. By owning several assets, certain types of risk (in particular specific risk) can be reduced.
Principal	In agency law, one under whose direction an agent acts and for whose benefit that agent acts is a principal.
Prototyping	An iterative approach to design in which a series of mock-ups or models are developed until the customer and the designer come to agreement as to the final design is called prototyping.
Controlling	A management function that involves determining whether or not an organization is progressing toward its goals and objectives, and taking corrective action if it is not is called controlling.

Go to **Cram101.com** for the Practice Tests for this Chapter.

Continuity	A media scheduling strategy where a continuous pattern of advertising is used over the time span of the advertising campaign is continuity.
Business opportunity	A business opportunity involves the sale or lease of any product, service, equipment, etc. that will enable the purchaser-licensee to begin a business
Critical success factor	Critical Success Factor is a business term for an element which is necessary for an organization or project to achieve its mission.
Success factor	The term success factor refers to the characteristics necessary for high performance; knowledge, skills, abilities, behaviors.
Balance	In banking and accountancy, the outstanding balance is the amount of money owned, (or due), that remains in a deposit account (or a loan account) at a given date, after all past remittances, payments and withdrawal have been accounted for. It can be positive (then, in the balance sheet of a firm, it is an asset) or negative (a liability).
Market	A market is, as defined in economics, a social arrangement that allows buyers and sellers to discover information and carry out a voluntary exchange of goods or services.
Core	A core is the set of feasible allocations in an economy that cannot be improved upon by subset of the set of the economy's consumers (a coalition). In construction, when the force in an element is within a certain center section, the core, the element will only be under compression.
Enterprise	Enterprise refers to another name for a business organization. Other similar terms are business firm, sometimes simply business, sometimes simply firm, as well as company, and entity.
Customer relationship management	Learning as much as possible about customers and doing everything you can to satisfy them or even delight them with goods and services over time is customer relationship management.
Relationship management	A method for developing long-term associations with customers is referred to as relationship management.
Management system	A management system is the framework of processes and procedures used to ensure that an organization can fulfill all tasks required to achieve its objectives.
Project management	Project management is the discipline of organizing and managing resources in such a way that these resources deliver all the work required to complete a project within defined scope, time, and cost constraints.
Business operations	Business operations are those activities involved in the running of a business for the purpose of producing value for the stakeholders. The outcome of business operations is the harvesting of value from assets owned by a business.
Comprehensive	A comprehensive refers to a layout accurate in size, color, scheme, and other necessary details to show how a final ad will look. For presentation only, never for reproduction.
Compromise	Compromise occurs when the interaction is moderately important to meeting goals and the goals are neither completely compatible nor completely incompatible.
Proprietary	Proprietary indicates that a party, or proprietor, exercises private ownership, control or use over an item of property, usually to the exclusion of other parties. Where a party, holds or claims proprietary interests in relation to certain types of property (eg. a creative literary work, or software), that property may also be the subject of intellectual property law (eg. copyright or patents).
Allowance	Reduction in the selling price of goods extended to the buyer because the goods are defective or of lower quality than the buyer ordered and to encourage a buyer to keep merchandise that

	would otherwise be returned is the allowance.
Overhead cost	An expenses of operating a business over and above the direct costs of producing a product is an overhead cost. They can include utilities (eg, electricity, telephone), advertizing and marketing, and any other costs not billed directly to the client or included in the price of the product.
Prototype	A prototype is built to test the function of a new design before starting production of a product.
Competitor	Other organizations in the same industry or type of business that provide a good or service to the same set of customers is referred to as a competitor.
Enterprise resource planning	Computer-based production and operations system that links multiple firms into one integrated production unit is enterprise resource planning.
Manufacturing	Production of goods primarily by the application of labor and capital to raw materials and other intermediate inputs, in contrast to agriculture, mining, forestry, fishing, and services a manufacturing.
Logistics	Those activities that focus on getting the right amount of the right products to the right place at the right time at the lowest possible cost is referred to as logistics.
Utility	Utility refers to the want-satisfying power of a good or service; the satisfaction or pleasure a consumer obtains from the consumption of a good or service.
Supply chain management	Supply chain management deals with the planning and execution issues involved in managing a supply chain. Supply chain management spans all movement and storage of raw materials, work-in-process inventory, and finished goods from point-of-origin to point-of-consumption.
Administration	Administration refers to the management and direction of the affairs of governments and institutions; a collective term for all policymaking officials of a government; the execution and implementation of public policy.
Supply chain	Supply chain refers to the flow of goods, services, and information from the initial sources of materials and services to the delivery of products to consumers.
Insurance	Insurance refers to a system by which individuals can reduce their exposure to risk of large losses by spreading the risks among a large number of persons.
Policy	Similar to a script in that a policy can be a less than completely rational decision-making method. Involves the use of a pre-existing set of decision steps for any problem that presents itself.
Electronic commerce	Electronic commerce or e-commerce, refers to any activity that uses some form of electronic communication in the inventory, exchange, advertisement, distribution, and payment of goods and services.
Business model	A business model is the instrument by which a business intends to generate revenue and profits. It is a summary of how a company means to serve its employees and customers, and involves both strategy (what an business intends to do) as well as an implementation.
Regulation	Regulation refers to restrictions state and federal laws place on business with regard to the conduct of its activities.
Adoption	In corporation law, a corporation's acceptance of a pre-incorporation contract by action of its board of directors, by which the corporation becomes liable on the contract, is referred to as adoption.
Commerce	Commerce is the exchange of something of value between two entities. It is the central

	mechanism from which capitalism is derived.
Default	In finance, default occurs when a debtor has not met its legal obligations according to the debt contract, e.g. it has not made a scheduled payment, or violated a covenant (condition) of the debt contract.
Scope	Scope of a project is the sum total of all projects products and their requirements or features.
Inventory	Tangible property held for sale in the normal course of business or used in producing goods or services for sale is an inventory.
Innovation	Innovation refers to the first commercially successful introduction of a new product, the use of a new method of production, or the creation of a new form of business organization.
Senior executive	Senior executive means a chief executive officer, chief operating officer, chief financial officer and anyone in charge of a principal business unit or function.
Gain	In finance, gain is a profit or an increase in value of an investment such as a stock or bond. Gain is calculated by fair market value or the proceeds from the sale of the investment minus the sum of the purchase price and all costs associated with it.
Foundation	A Foundation is a type of philanthropic organization set up by either individuals or institutions as a legal entity (either as a corporation or trust) with the purpose of distributing grants to support causes in line with the goals of the foundation.
Business unit	The lowest level of the company which contains the set of functions that carry a product through its life span from concept through manufacture, distribution, sales and service is a business unit.
Corporation	A legal entity chartered by a state or the Federal government that is distinct and separate from the individuals who own it is a corporation. This separation gives the corporation unique powers which other legal entities lack.
Business strategy	Business strategy, which refers to the aggregated operational strategies of single business firm or that of an SBU in a diversified corporation refers to the way in which a firm competes in its chosen arenas.
Organizational structure	Organizational structure is the way in which the interrelated groups of an organization are constructed. From a managerial point of view the main concerns are ensuring effective communication and coordination.
Productivity	Productivity refers to the total output of goods and services in a given period of time divided by work hours.
Rapid application development	Rapid application development is a software programming technique that allows quick development of software applications. Some rapid application development implementations include visual tools for development and others generate software frameworks through tools known as "wizards".
Groupware	Software application that enables multiple users to track, share, and organize information and to work on the same database or document simultaneously is the groupware.
Intranet	Intranet refers to a companywide network, closed to public access, that uses Internet-type technology. A set of communications links within one company that travel over the Internet but are closed to public access.
Organization structure	The system of task, reporting, and authority relationships within which the organization does its work is referred to as the organization structure.
Economics	The social science dealing with the use of scarce resources to obtain the maximum

	satisfaction of society's virtually unlimited economic wants is an economics.
Automation	Automation allows machines to do work previously accomplished by people.
Unit cost	Unit cost refers to cost computed by dividing some amount of total costs by the related number of units. Also called average cost.
Workflow	Workflow refers to automated systems that electronically route documents to the next person in the process.
Cost structure	The relative proportion of an organization's fixed, variable, and mixed costs is referred to as cost structure.
Value chain	The sequence of business functions in which usefulness is added to the products or services of a company is a value chain.
Management team	A management team is directly responsible for managing the day-to-day operations (and profitability) of a company.
International firm	International firm refers to those firms who have responded to stiff competition domestically by expanding their sales abroad. They may start a production facility overseas and send some of their managers, who report to a global division, to that country.
Synergy	Corporate synergy occurs when corporations interact congruently. A corporate synergy refers to a financial benefit that a corporation expects to realize when it merges with or acquires another corporation.
Purchasing	Purchasing refers to the function in a firm that searches for quality material resources, finds the best suppliers, and negotiates the best price for goods and services.
License	A license in the sphere of Intellectual Property Rights (IPR) is a document, contract or agreement giving permission or the 'right' to a legally-definable entity to do something (such as manufacture a product or to use a service), or to apply something (such as a trademark), with the objective of achieving commercial gain.
Capital	Capital generally refers to financial wealth, especially that used to start or maintain a business. In classical economics, capital is one of four factors of production, the others being land and labor and entrepreneurship.
Attachment	Attachment in general, the process of taking a person's property under an appropriate judicial order by an appropriate officer of the court. Used for a variety of purposes, including the acquisition of jurisdiction over the property seized and the securing of property that may be used to satisfy a debt.
Revenue	Revenue is a U.S. business term for the amount of money that a company receives from its activities, mostly from sales of products and/or services to customers.
Accumulation	The acquisition of an increasing quantity of something. The accumulation of factors, especially capital, is a primary mechanism for economic growth.
Interest	In finance and economics, interest is the price paid by a borrower for the use of a lender's money. In other words, interest is the amount of paid to "rent" money for a period of time.
Authority	Authority in agency law, refers to an agent's ability to affect his principal's legal relations with third parties. Also used to refer to an actor's legal power or ability to do something. In addition, sometimes used to refer to a statute, case, or other legal source that justifies a particular result.
Argument	The discussion by counsel for the respective parties of their contentions on the law and the facts of the case being tried in order to aid the jury in arriving at a correct and just conclusion is called argument.

Go to **Cram101.com** for the Practice Tests for this Chapter.

Channel	Channel, in communications (sometimes called communications channel), refers to the medium used to convey information from a sender (or transmitter) to a receiver.
Trust	An arrangement in which shareholders of independent firms agree to give up their stock in exchange for trust certificates that entitle them to a share of the trust's common profits.
Preference	The act of a debtor in paying or securing one or more of his creditors in a manner more favorable to them than to other creditors or to the exclusion of such other creditors is a preference. In the absence of statute, a preference is perfectly good, but to be legal it must be bona fide, and not a mere subterfuge of the debtor to secure a future benefit to himself or to prevent the application of his property to his debts.
Intervention	Intervention refers to an activity in which a government buys or sells its currency in the foreign exchange market in order to affect its currency's exchange rate.
Conglomerate	A conglomerate is a large company that consists of divisions of often seemingly unrelated businesses.
Maturity	Maturity refers to the final payment date of a loan or other financial instrument, after which point no further interest or principal need be paid.
Centralization	A structural policy in which decision-making authority is concentrated at the top of the organizational hierarchy is referred to as centralization.
General Motors	General Motors is the world's largest automaker. Founded in 1908, today it employs about 327,000 people around the world. With global headquarters in Detroit, it manufactures its cars and trucks in 33 countries.
Subsidiary	A company that is controlled by another company or corporation is a subsidiary.
Equity	Equity is the name given to the set of legal principles, in countries following the English common law tradition, which supplement strict rules of law where their application would operate harshly, so as to achieve what is sometimes referred to as "natural justice."
Profit	Profit refers to the return to the resource entrepreneurial ability; total revenue minus total cost.
Active management	Active management refers to a portfolio management strategy where the manager makes specific investments with the goal of outperforming a benchmark index. Ideally, the manager exploits market inefficiencies by selecting securities that are undervalued. Depending on the goals of the specific investment portfolio or mutual fund, active management may also strive to achieve a goal of less volatility or risk than the benchmark index instead of, or in addition to, greater long-term return.
Subcontract	A subcontract is a contract that assigns part of an existing contract to a different party.
Restructuring	Restructuring is the corporate management term for the act of partially dismantling and reorganizing a company for the purpose of making it more efficient and therefore more profitable.
Leverage	Leverage is using given resources in such a way that the potential positive or negative outcome is magnified. In finance, this generally refers to borrowing.
Appeal	Appeal refers to the act of asking an appellate court to overturn a decision after the trial court's final judgment has been entered.
Credit	Credit refers to a recording as positive in the balance of payments, any transaction that gives rise to a payment into the country, such as an export, the sale of an asset, or borrowing from abroad.
Churn	Churn is the process by which jobs are regularly created and destroyed as technology changes.

Go to **Cram101.com** for the Practice Tests for this Chapter.

Competitive Strategy	An outline of how a business intends to compete with other firms in the same industry is called competitive strategy.
Organizational culture	The mindset of employees, including their shared beliefs, values, and goals is called the organizational culture.
Strategic intent	Strategic intent is when a firm relentlessly pursues a difficult strategic goa and concentrates its competitive actions and energies on achieving that goal.
Incentive	An incentive is any factor (financial or non-financial) that provides a motive for a particular course of action, or counts as a reason for preferring one choice to the alternatives.
Economies of scale	In economics, returns to scale and economies of scale are related terms that describe what happens as the scale of production increases. They are different terms and not to be used interchangeably.
Cost efficiency	Cost efficiency refers to the amount of output associated with an additional dollar spent on input; the MPP of an input divided by its price. Also refers to is a ratio of the excess return over a fund's benchmark, divided by management expenses. It calculates the value added (i.e. the excess over index returns) contributed by each percentage point of management expenses.
Economy	The income, expenditures, and resources that affect the cost of running a business and household are called an economy.
Discount	The difference between the face value of a bond and its selling price, when a bond is sold for less than its face value it's referred to as a discount.
Shareholder	A shareholder is an individual or company (including a corporation) that legally owns one or more shares of stock in a joined stock company.
Licensing	Licensing is a form of strategic alliance which involves the sale of a right to use certain proprietary knowledge (so called intellectual property) in a defined way.
Marketing	Promoting and selling products or services to customers, or prospective customers, is referred to as marketing.
Bid	A bid price is a price offered by a buyer when he/she buys a good. In the context of stock trading on a stock exchange, the bid price is the highest price a buyer of a stock is willing to pay for a share of that given stock.
Alignment	Term that refers to optimal coordination among disparate departments and divisions within a firm is referred to as alignment.
Sourcing decisions	Whether a firm should make or buy component parts are sourcing decisions.
Mistake	In contract law a mistake is incorrect understanding by one or more parties to a contract and may be used as grounds to invalidate the agreement. Common law has identified three different types of mistake in contract: unilateral mistake, mutual mistake, and common mistake.
Market price	Market price is an economic concept with commonplace familiarity; it is the price that a good or service is offered at, or will fetch, in the marketplace; it is of interest mainly in the study of microeconomics.
Amoco	Amoco was formed as Standard Oil (Indiana) in 1889 by John D. Rockefeller as part of the Standard Oil trust. In 1910, with the rise in popularity of the automobile, Amoco decided to specialize in providing gas to everyday families and their cars. In 1911, the year it became independent from the Standard Oil trust, the company sold 88% of the gasoline and kerosene sold in the midwest.

Go to **Cram101.com** for the Practice Tests for this Chapter.

Verification	Verification refers to the final stage of the creative process where the validity or truthfulness of the insight is determined. The feedback portion of communication in which the receiver sends a message to the source indicating receipt of the message and the degree to which he or she understood the message.
Termination	The ending of a corporation that occurs only after the winding-up of the corporation's affairs, the liquidation of its assets, and the distribution of the proceeds to the claimants are referred to as a termination.
Committee	A long-lasting, sometimes permanent team in the organization structure created to deal with tasks that recur regularly is the committee.
Arbitrate	To submit some disputed matter to selected persons and to accept their decision or award as a substitute for the decision of a judicial tribunal is called the arbitrate.
Payback	A value that indicates the time period required to recoup an initial investment is a payback. The payback does not include the time-value-of-money concept.
Application service provider	An application service provider is a business that provides computer-based services to customers over a network.
Convergence	The blending of various facets of marketing functions and communication technology to create more efficient and expanded synergies is a convergence.
Lease	A contract for the possession and use of land or other property, including goods, on one side, and a recompense of rent or other income on the other is the lease.
Property	Assets defined in the broadest legal sense. Property includes the unrealized receivables of a cash basis taxpayer, but not services rendered.
Security	Security refers to a claim on the borrower future income that is sold by the borrower to the lender. A security is a type of transferable interest representing financial value.
Recovery	Characterized by rizing output, falling unemployment, rizing profits, and increasing economic activity following a decline is a recovery.
Privilege	Generally, a legal right to engage in conduct that would otherwise result in legal liability is a privilege. Privileges are commonly classified as absolute or conditional. Occasionally, privilege is also used to denote a legal right to refrain from particular behavior.
Invoice	The itemized bill for a transaction, stating the nature of the transaction and its cost. In international trade, the invoice price is often the preferred basis for levying an ad valorem tariff.
Financial risk	The risk related to the inability of the firm to meet its debt obligations as they come due is called financial risk.
Sun Microsystems	Sun Microsystems is most well known for its Unix systems, which have a reputation for system stability and a consistent design philosophy.
Scientific management	Studying workers to find the most efficient ways of doing things and then teaching people those techniques is scientific management.
Retailing	All activities involved in selling, renting, and providing goods and services to ultimate consumers for personal, family, or household use is referred to as retailing.
Servqual	A survey instrument designed to assess service quality along five specific dimensions consisting of tangibles, reliability, responsiveness, assurance, and empathy is referred to as servqual.
Insourcing	Insourcing refers to process of producing goods or providing services within the organization

Go to **Cram101.com** for the Practice Tests for this Chapter.

	rather than purchasing those same goods or services from outside vendors.
Best practice	Best practice is a management idea which asserts that there is a technique, method, process, activity, incentive or reward that is more effective at delivering a particular outcome than any other technique, method, process, etc.
Management information system	A computer-based system that provides information and support for effective managerial decision makin is referred to as a management information system.
Public sector	Public sector refers to the part of the economy that contains all government entities; government.
Mitigation	A nonbreaching party that is under a legal duty to avoid or reduce damages caused by a breach of contract is a mitigation.

Information technology	Information technology refers to technology that helps companies change business by allowing them to use new methods.
Technology	The body of knowledge and techniques that can be used to combine economic resources to produce goods and services is called technology.
Management	Management characterizes the process of leading and directing all or part of an organization, often a business, through the deployment and manipulation of resources. Early twentieth-century management writer Mary Parker Follett defined management as "the art of getting things done through people."
Investment	Investment refers to spending for the production and accumulation of capital and additions to inventories. In a financial sense, buying an asset with the expectation of making a return.
Acceleration	Acceleration refers to the shortening of the time for the performance of a contract or the payment of a note by the operation of some provision in the contract or note itself.
Productivity	Productivity refers to the total output of goods and services in a given period of time divided by work hours.
Gain	In finance, gain is a profit or an increase in value of an investment such as a stock or bond. Gain is calculated by fair market value or the proceeds from the sale of the investment minus the sum of the purchase price and all costs associated with it.
Business process	Business process refers to the individual activities of an enterprise. Processes can be viewed at a high level, for example, 'marketing,' or at the level of detailed subprocesses, for example, 'customer retention.'.
Management team	A management team is directly responsible for managing the day-to-day operations (and profitability) of a company.
Context	The effect of the background under which a message often takes on more and richer meaning is a context. Context is especially important in cross-cultural interactions because some cultures are said to be high context or low context.
Controlling	A management function that involves determining whether or not an organization is progressing toward its goals and objectives, and taking corrective action if it is not is called controlling.
Firm	An organization that employs resources to produce a good or service for profit and owns and operates one or more plants is referred to as a firm.
Industry	A group of firms that produce identical or similar products is an industry. It is also used specifically to refer to an area of economic production focused on manufacturing which involves large amounts of capital investment before any profit can be realized, also called "heavy industry".
Economy	The income, expenditures, and resources that affect the cost of running a business and household are called an economy.
Competitive advantage	A business is said to have a competitive advantage when its unique strengths, often based on cost, quality, time, and innovation, offer consumers a greater percieved value and there by differtiating it from its competitors.
Information system	An information system is a system whether automated or manual, that comprises people, machines, and/or methods organized to collect, process, transmit, and disseminate data that represent user information.
Competitive disadvantage	A situation in which a firm is not implementing using strategies that are being used by competing organizations is competitive disadvantage.

215

Business strategy	Business strategy, which refers to the aggregated operational strategies of single business firm or that of an SBU in a diversified corporation refers to the way in which a firm competes in its chosen arenas.
Option	A contract that gives the purchaser the option to buy or sell the underlying financial instrument at a specified price, called the exercise price or strike price, within a specific period of time.
Contribution	In business organization law, the cash or property contributed to a business by its owners is referred to as contribution.
Continuous process	An uninterrupted production process in which long production runs turn out finished goods over time is called continuous process.
Brief	Brief refers to a statement of a party's case or legal arguments, usually prepared by an attorney. Also used to make legal arguments before appellate courts.
Strategic management	A philosophy of management that links strategic planning with dayto-day decision making. Strategic management seeks a fit between an organization's external and internal environments.
Strategic planning	The process of determining the major goals of the organization and the policies and strategies for obtaining and using resources to achieve those goals is called strategic planning.
Strategy formulation	The process of deciding on a strategic direction by defining a company's mission and goals, its external opportunities and threats, and its internal strengths and weaknesses is referred to as a strategy formulation.
Integration	Economic integration refers to reducing barriers among countries to transactions and to movements of goods, capital, and labor, including harmonization of laws, regulations, and standards. Integrated markets theoretically function as a unified market.
Organizational structure	Organizational structure is the way in which the interrelated groups of an organization are constructed. From a managerial point of view the main concerns are ensuring effective communication and coordination.
Service	Service refers to a "non tangible product" that is not embodied in a physical good and that typically effects some change in another product, person, or institution. Contrasts with good.
Alignment	Term that refers to optimal coordination among disparate departments and divisions within a firm is referred to as alignment.
Competitor	Other organizations in the same industry or type of business that provide a good or service to the same set of customers is referred to as a competitor.
Market	A market is, as defined in economics, a social arrangement that allows buyers and sellers to discover information and carry out a voluntary exchange of goods or services.
Innovation	Innovation refers to the first commercially successful introduction of a new product, the use of a new method of production, or the creation of a new form of business organization.
Inputs	The inputs used by a firm or an economy are the labor, raw materials, electricity and other resources it uses to produce its outputs.
Portfolio	In finance, a portfolio is a collection of investments held by an institution or a private individual. Holding but not always a portfolio is part of an investment and risk-limiting strategy called diversification. By owning several assets, certain types of risk (in particular specific risk) can be reduced.

Go to **Cram101.com** for the Practice Tests for this Chapter.

Go to **Cram101.com** for the Practice Tests for this Chapter.
And, **NEVER** highlight a book again!

Portfolio approach	Portfolio approach refers to an approach to explaining exchange rates that stresses their role in changing the proportions of different currency-denominated assets in portfolios. The exchange rate adjusts to equate these proportions to desired levels.
Senior management	Senior management is generally a team of individuals at the highest level of organizational management who have the day-to-day responsibilities of managing a corporation.
Compromise	Compromise occurs when the interaction is moderately important to meeting goals and the goals are neither completely compatible nor completely incompatible.
Supply	Supply is the aggregate amount of any material good that can be called into being at a certain price point; it comprises one half of the equation of supply and demand. In classical economic theory, a curve representing supply is one of the factors that produce price.
Business development	Business development emcompasses a number of techniques designed to grow an economic enterprise. Such techniques include, but are not limited to, assessments of marketing opportunities and target markets, intelligence gathering on customers and competitors, generating leads for possible sales, followup sales activity, and formal proposal writing.
Balance	In banking and accountancy, the outstanding balance is the amount of money owned, (or due), that remains in a deposit account (or a loan account) at a given date, after all past remittances, payments and withdrawal have been accounted for. It can be positive (then, in the balance sheet of a firm, it is an asset) or negative (a liability).
Enabling	Enabling refers to giving workers the education and tools they need to assume their new decision-making powers.
Organization development	The process of planned change and improvement of the organization through application of knowledge of the behavioral sciences is called organization development.
Complexity	The technical sophistication of the product and hence the amount of understanding required to use it is referred to as complexity. It is the opposite of simplicity.
Complement	A good that is used in conjunction with another good is a complement. For example, cameras and film would complement eachother.
Assessment	Collecting information and providing feedback to employees about their behavior, communication style, or skills is an assessment.
Drucker	Drucker as a business thinker took off in the 1940s, when his initial writings on politics and society won him access to the internal workings of General Motors, which was one of the largest companies in the world at that time. His experiences in Europe had left him fascinated with the problem of authority.
Downsizing	The process of eliminating managerial and non-managerial positions are called downsizing.
Specialist	A specialist is a trader who makes a market in one or several stocks and holds the limit order book for those stocks.
Economics	The social science dealing with the use of scarce resources to obtain the maximum satisfaction of society's virtually unlimited economic wants is an economics.
Scope	Scope of a project is the sum total of all projects products and their requirements or features.
Capital	Capital generally refers to financial wealth, especially that used to start or maintain a business. In classical economics, capital is one of four factors of production, the others being land and labor and entrepreneurship.
Demographic	A demographic is a term used in marketing and broadcasting, to describe a demographic grouping or a market segment.

Go to **Cram101.com** for the Practice Tests for this Chapter.

Allocate	Allocate refers to the assignment of income for various tax purposes. A multistate corporation's nonbusiness income usually is distributed to the state where the nonbusiness assets are located; it is not apportioned with the rest of the entity's income.
Core	A core is the set of feasible allocations in an economy that cannot be improved upon by subset of the set of the economy's consumers (a coalition). In construction, when the force in an element is within a certain center section, the core, the element will only be under compression.
Organization structure	The system of task, reporting, and authority relationships within which the organization does its work is referred to as the organization structure.
Consideration	Consideration in contract law, a basic requirement for an enforceable agreement under traditional contract principles, defined in this text as legal value, bargained for and given in exchange for an act or promise. In corporation law, cash or property contributed to a corporation in exchange for shares, or a promise to contribute such cash or property.
Personnel	A collective term for all of the employees of an organization. Personnel is also commonly used to refer to the personnel management function or the organizational unit responsible for administering personnel programs.
Corporation	A legal entity chartered by a state or the Federal government that is distinct and separate from the individuals who own it is a corporation. This separation gives the corporation unique powers which other legal entities lack.
Asset	An item of property, such as land, capital, money, a share in ownership, or a claim on others for future payment, such as a bond or a bank deposit is an asset.
Product innovation	The development and sale of a new or improved product is a product innovation. Production of a new product on a commercial basis.
Value chain	The sequence of business functions in which usefulness is added to the products or services of a company is a value chain.
Extension	Extension refers to an out-of-court settlement in which creditors agree to allow the firm more time to meet its financial obligations. A new repayment schedule will be developed, subject to the acceptance of creditors.
Globalization	The increasing world-wide integration of markets for goods, services and capital that attracted special attention in the late 1990s is called globalization.
Channel	Channel, in communications (sometimes called communications channel), refers to the medium used to convey information from a sender (or transmitter) to a receiver.
Exchange	The trade of things of value between buyer and seller so that each is better off after the trade is called the exchange.
Stakeholder	A stakeholder is an individual or group with a vested interest in or expectation for organizational performance. Usually stakeholders can either have an effect on or are affected by an organization.
Asset management	Asset management is the method that a company uses to track fixed assets, for example factory equipment, desks and chairs, computers, even buildings. Although the exact details of the task varies widely from company to company, asset management often includes tracking the physical location of assets, managing demand for scarce resources, and accounting tasks such as amortization.
Performance improvement	Performance improvement is the concept of measuring the output of a particular process or procedure then modifying the process or procedure in order to increase the output, increase efficiency, or increase the effectiveness of the process or procedure.

Go to **Cram101.com** for the Practice Tests for this Chapter.

Corporate policy	Dimension of social responsibility that refers to the position a firm takes on social and political issues is referred to as corporate policy.
Policy	Similar to a script in that a policy can be a less than completely rational decision-making method. Involves the use of a pre-existing set of decision steps for any problem that presents itself.
Change management	Change management is the process of developing a planned approach to change in an organization. Typically the objective is to maximize the collective benefits for all people involved in the change and minimize the risk of failure of implementing the change.
Respondent	Respondent refers to a term often used to describe the party charged in an administrative proceeding. The party adverse to the appellant in a case appealed to a higher court.
Reorganization	Reorganization occurs, among other instances, when one corporation acquires another in a merger or acquisition, a single corporation divides into two or more entities, or a corporation makes a substantial change in its capital structure.
Investment management	Investment management is a branch of investment analysis that looks into the process of managing money. Investment portfolios can be managed through decisions about security purchases and sales.
Supply and demand	The partial equilibrium supply and demand economic model originally developed by Alfred Marshall attempts to describe, explain, and predict changes in the price and quantity of goods sold in competitive markets.
Matching	Matching refers to an accounting concept that establishes when expenses are recognized. Expenses are matched with the revenues they helped to generate and are recognized when those revenues are recognized.
Customer relationship management	Learning as much as possible about customers and doing everything you can to satisfy them or even delight them with goods and services over time is customer relationship management.
Relationship management	A method for developing long-term associations with customers is referred to as relationship management.
Economic analysis	The process of deriving economic principles from relevant economic facts are called economic analysis. It is the comparison, with money as the index, of those costs and benefits to the wider economy that can be reasonably quantified, including all social costs and benefits of a project.
Paradox	As used in economics, paradox means something unexpected, rather than the more extreme normal meaning of something seemingly impossible. Some paradoxes are just theoretical results that go against what one thinks of as normal.
Variable	A variable is something measured by a number; it is used to analyze what happens to other things when the size of that number changes.
Business value	Business value is an informal term that includes all forms of value that determine the health and well-being of the firm in the long-run.
Value creation	Value creation refers to performing activities that increase the value of goods or services to consumers.
Organizational performance	Organizational performance comprises the actual output or results of an organization as measured against its intended outputs (or goals and objectives).
Yield	The interest rate that equates a future value or an annuity to a given present value is a yield.

223

Budget	Budget refers to an account, usually for a year, of the planned expenditures and the expected receipts of an entity. For a government, the receipts are tax revenues.
Manufacturing	Production of goods primarily by the application of labor and capital to raw materials and other intermediate inputs, in contrast to agriculture, mining, forestry, fishing, and services a manufacturing.
Analogy	Analogy is either the cognitive process of transferring information from a particular subject to another particular subject (the target), or a linguistic expression corresponding to such a process. In a narrower sense, analogy is an inference or an argument from a particular to another particular, as opposed to deduction, induction, and abduction, where at least one of the premises or the conclusion is general.
Open market	In economics, the open market is the term used to refer to the environment in which bonds are bought and sold.
Proprietary	Proprietary indicates that a party, or proprietor, exercises private ownership, control or use over an item of property, usually to the exclusion of other parties. Where a party, holds or claims proprietary interests in relation to certain types of property (eg. a creative literary work, or software), that property may also be the subject of intellectual property law (eg. copyright or patents).
Knowledge base	Knowledge base refers to a database that includes decision rules for use of the data, which may be qualitative as well as quantitative.
Points	Loan origination fees that may be deductible as interest by a buyer of property. A seller of property who pays points reduces the selling price by the amount of the points paid for the buyer.
Grant	Grant refers to an intergovernmental transfer of funds . Since the New Deal, state and local governments have become increasingly dependent upon federal grants for an almost infinite variety of programs.
Outsourcing	Outsourcing refers to a production activity that was previously done inside a firm or plant that is now conducted outside that firm or plant.
Realization	Realization is the sale of assets when an entity is being liquidated.
Leverage	Leverage is using given resources in such a way that the potential positive or negative outcome is magnified. In finance, this generally refers to borrowing.
Human resource management	The process of evaluating human resource needs, finding people to fill those needs, and getting the best work from each employee by providing the right incentives and job environment, all with the goal of meeting the needs of the firm are called human resource management.
Resource management	Resource management is the efficient and effective deployment of an organization's resources when they are needed. Such resources may include financial resources, inventory, human skills, production resources, or information technology.
Aptitude	An aptitude is an innate inborn ability to do a certain kind of work. Aptitudes may be physical or mental. Many of them have been identified and are testable.
Empathy	Empathy refers to dimension of service quality-caring individualized attention provided to customers.
Users	Users refer to people in the organization who actually use the product or service purchased by the buying center.
Functional organization	Functional organization is a method of organization in which chapters and sections of a manual correspond to business functions, not specific departments or work groups.

Go to **Cram101.com** for the Practice Tests for this Chapter.

Business operations	Business operations are those activities involved in the running of a business for the purpose of producing value for the stakeholders. The outcome of business operations is the harvesting of value from assets owned by a business.
Operation	A standardized method or technique that is performed repetitively, often on different materials resulting in different finished goods is called an operation.
Reinsurance	An allocation of the portion of the insurance risk to another company in exchange for a portion of the insurance premium is called reinsurance.
Board of directors	The group of individuals elected by the stockholders of a corporation to oversee its operations is a board of directors.
Partnership	In the common law, a partnership is a type of business entity in which partners share with each other the profits or losses of the business undertaking in which they have all invested.
Stock market	An organized marketplace in which common stocks are traded. In the United States, the largest stock market is the New York Stock Exchange, on which are traded the stocks of the largest U.S. companies.
Stock	In financial terminology, stock is the capital raized by a corporation, through the issuance and sale of shares.
Hierarchy	A system of grouping people in an organization according to rank from the top down in which all subordinate managers must report to one person is called a hierarchy.
Interdependence	The extent to which departments depend on each other for resources or materials to accomplish their tasks is referred to as interdependence.
Journal	Book of original entry, in which transactions are recorded in a general ledger system, is referred to as a journal.
Financial market	In economics, a financial market is a mechanism which allows people to trade money for securities or commodities such as gold or other precious metals. In general, any commodity market might be considered to be a financial market, if the usual purpose of traders is not the immediate consumption of the commodity, but rather as a means of delaying or accelerating consumption over time.

Go to **Cram101.com** for the Practice Tests for this Chapter.

658.4038 CRA

N/L

C4